Easy As 123	2
Building Your Dream	4
Perfecting Your Plans	8
Custom Home	11
Specifying your Dream	14
Financial Matters	17
How your Lumber Dealer Can Help You	20
Building Your Home Month By Month	21
Design America Designers	22
Interiors	26
Order Form	33
Home Plan Features	34 – 224

Whether You're a First-Time Home Builder or an Experienced Contractor...

...Design America's exceptional home plans and helpful, knowledgeable staff will make your project a complete success!

◆ ◆ ◆

1 Choose the Design America Home Plan Book that offers plans for the style of home you've always wanted.

The plans in our Design America Series have been created by many of the nation's top architects and designers. No matter what your tastes, you're sure to find several homes you would be thrilled to call your own.

You can select from a wide range of styles, including the hottest new trends in contemporary styling. Design America has them all! We also showcase outstanding plans of affordable homes for those who are building on a budget.

In addition to more than 200 home plans included in each Design America book, you'll find a wealth of other helpful information. Companion articles will give you hints on securing construction financing and show you how easy and inexpensive it is to customize your plans.

Order a complete set of blueprints.

Design America plans provide you with a complete blueprint package from as low as **$195.00. Blueprints include the following:**

- Exterior elevations of all sides

- Foundation plans and details

- Scaled floor plans

- Locations of electrical outlets, switches & light fixtures

- Plumbing schematic plan (If available)

- Roof & wall sections

- Cross-section view

- Material list and general notes (If available)

It's reassuring to know that Design America's blueprints meet one or more nationally recognized building standards at the time and place they were drawn. If you'd like a preview of one of our home designs, ask us about a Preview Plan of the home. Some plans offer a Preview Plan that shows the exterior elevation drawings of the plan, the floor plan, and kitchen cabinet elevations.

Customize the blueprints you select for a tailor-made home just for you.

From changing siding material to adding a walk-in closet or a room, our design staff will save you thousands of dollars over what you might otherwise pay. For a nominal charge, we can even mirror-reverse the entire plan!

In addition to design customization, Design America also provides assistance in securing construction financing. **Call us today** and we'll be happy to give you more information on this helpful, time saving service.

Our #1 goal is to help you build the home that matches your needs and lifestyle.

Call us toll free **(800) 533-4350** or fax us your blueprint order today at **(800) 344-4293.** Let's get started on your new home!

Real Life Home-Building Experiences

Are you wondering what it's like to build your own home?

Let those who have gone before you share what they have learned.

◆ ◆ ◆

If you're apprehensive about tackling such a huge project as building your own home (and who wouldn't be?), take heart. People of all levels of experience and backgrounds have successfully built homes for themselves. There are many ways to achieve your goal of a custom-built home. If you wish to avoid as many headaches as possible, hiring an experienced builder to handle all the details is the answer. If you possess a lot of confidence and have the desire to save as much money as possible, acting as your own general contractor is the way to go. There are even those who use a blended approach, hiring a builder to take care of some tasks, and completing the rest themselves. In all cases, the key to success is to do your homework. Doing the proper research first helps to minimize problems down the road. Part of that research is understanding the mistakes others have made so you can learn from them.

Playing the Role of the General Contractor

When you are the general contractor on your home building project, you can expect to have more challenges to deal with than if you hire a builder. Those who have lived through the experience have learned, however, that the snags aren't insurmountable. Sometimes these challenges can be turned into positives and **you can save a lot of money.**

Chuck Weidner, of rural Harvard, Ill. is a repeat customer of National Plan Service USA,Inc. Twenty years ago he used plans from NPS to build a home in suburban Chicago. In April 1993 he and his wife Annette, following a set of Design America plans, started construction on another home situated on ten acres near the Wisconsin state line. They chose the design, a truly grand Victorian home encompassing over 2,500 square feet with an enormous porch that wraps

around more than half of the house. Chuck and Annette are proof that you can play the role of general contractor if you're willing to endure some difficulties. Together, they served as the general contractor on both homes.

Other than five years working in construction (he's a police officer now), Chuck had no experience as a general contractor prior to building the first home. He and Annette taught themselves as they went through the process. What was the most trying part of the whole experience? "Making sure that all the subcontractors got their work done on time," answers Chuck. "Personality conflicts between the subcontractors was the biggest challenge. For example, the carpenters weren't happy with the way the electrician's were doing their work. The sheetrock was delivered at the same same the insulators were here, and it caused some difficulties…you just need to talk to both of them and make some compromises."

Chuck and Annette had the misfortune of buying their lumber shortly after Hurricane Andrew hit southern Florida in the fall of 1992. The demand for lumber for rebuilding caused prices to skyrocket. "The first time we went for bids was in September," explains Chuck, "and then we didn't really finalize it until January or February. The price of just the lumber went up $12,000…that was something we did not plan on."

Despite these problems, work progressed smoothly. The Weidners didn't need to alter their house plans to get the village's approval. There were no construction delays, even for the weather, and the project was completed on schedule. The solution to one particular problem turned out to augment the design of their house. The excavators and laborers were having trouble installing the septic tank because of the slope of the ground. "They had to move the house 15 or 20 feet," explains Chuck, "and that raised the foundation in the back where we now have a walk-out basement."

Chuck & Annette Weidner

Weidner Residence   Photo courtesy of Carl Cullen

When you are your own general contractor, finding a construction loan can also be difficult. Banks are hesitant to lend if an experienced builder isn't involved. "We looked at a few banks," says Chuck, "but they all wanted to see a builder." The Weidners eventually financed the construction of their latest home with a home equity loan taken out on their old house.

"The most enjoyable part of the whole experience was seeing everything coming together," says Chuck, "Towards the end, when all the goodies come in such as the trim, cabinets, and flooring...then it starts looking like a house." Another positive outcome was the money Chuck and Annette saved by not hiring a builder. They **estimate their savings totalled $40,000.**

Would he recommend that anyone try being a general contractor? "I would say yes. With a little guidance from someone that's in the trades who knows what the difficulties are...I think anybody can do it." What advice would he give someone who's considering such an undertaking? "Make sure you're work-ing with reputable people, get several bids, and check with the county where you get your permits, because they can make helpful recommendations (when looking for subcontractors)." Chuck mentioned that negotiation skills are also helpful when dealing with the trades.

Obviously, if asked if they would do it again, Chuck and Annette's answer would be

yes. And, they would use Design America plans. The Weidners were so impressed with the quality of the plans and service they received that they have recommended Design America plans to other people.

Hiring A Builder

Serving as your own general contractor involves managing all aspects of your home-building project. Building materials must be ordered, and competitive bids must be solicited. A complete work schedule must be created, and deliveries and subcontractors' work must be coordinated. In addition, you have to make sure that the subcontractors (or trades as they are also known) get paid on time so that no mechanic's liens are put on your property. Make sure the necessary building permits and insurance are in place, and it's your responsibility that the plans for your house get approved by the village building authority.

If this sounds too overwhelming, consider hiring a local builder to do this work for you. The builder will take care of as much of the project as you want. If you decide to hire a builder, finding a reliable one is essential. How do you go about finding a reputable builder? And what separates the good builders from the bad ones?

"Word of mouth is the best way to find a builder," says Eric Rossi of Avanti Construction Corp., a builder based in the near west suburbs of Chicago. Rossi has been in the business for 20 years and builds 10 to 15 hous-es per year in Chicago's western and north-western suburbs. He recently used a set of Design America plans for one of his homes and was very pleased with the result. "Talk to peo-ple. See some spec homes. Go in and see the type of work their doing. Talk to people who have bought their homes and ask them what they think of their house," Ross recommends.

There are various third party sources that you can check out as well. Local attorneys and county offices should be able to provide you with information about the track record of a particular builder. Reporting services such as Dun & Bradstreet can be consulted as well. One especially important item to investigate is whether or not the builders pay their subcontractors on schedule. A sub who doesn't get paid on schedule can place a mechanic's lien on your property preventing you from calling it your own until he gets paid. Every builder has had to fend off mechanic's liens at one time or another, however, the fact that a builder has a few doesn't necessarily mean he isn't doing his job. "That's one of the problems in the business," says Rossi. "Any guy that has a dispute can throw a lien on you. There should be some guidelines, there should be some standards that they have to meet, But there's nothing like that." A builder with many liens from several different subs should raise a red flag. A good builder will avoid all but the most frivolous liens. "I don't let things slide. My tradespeople perform and they get paid, and that's important," Rossi states.

It's a good idea to research and hire your builder early, while you're still in the planning stages, and even before your house plans are finalized. This is important because the builder will offer many helpful suggestions concerning the plans and specs. When it comes time to start construction, the builder may know of a more efficient or cost-effective way to achieve a certain result. The builder can also tell you if there are going to be any problems getting the village's approval for the plans. Good builders will always be doing research and attending trade shows to stay informed on the latest issues in the industry. You should tap into this knowledge as early in the process as possible.

Rossi points out that if your home's interior will be completed during the colder months, your labor costs will be less. This is because less construction takes place during the winter and so there are more plumbers, electricians, etc. available. With more trades competing for fewer jobs, they'll be more likely to offer discounted rates during winter.

Builders such as Rossi have built homes for many people and are full of helpful hints. Rossi recommends locating your financing first, before doing anything else. "The first thing to do is to find out what you're qualified for. You don't want to be looking for a $300,000 home if you've only qualified for $170,000. Then your next step is to find your land." Rossi recommends finding a lot in a location you like and then picking out house plans that fit the lot. Don't select your plans before the lot, and allow enough time for construction. "You've got to figure six to eight months to build a house even though everybody wants it in three," says Rossi.

The best piece of advice that Rossi can give to those building their own home is to choose your builder carefully. Shop around and select a builder based on reputation and the quality of their work.

It's Definitely Worth Building Yourself to Get Exactly What You Want.

Having owned half a dozen different houses and condos, Bob and Judy Sipek decided to build a custom home in a southwestern suburb of Chicago. Bob works as a project manager and Judy is a building manager. "We wanted a new home and so we found a lot we really liked in a nice subdivision and started looking for house plans and a builder," explains Bob. "We ended up going with the builder who built my sister's house because I could see he did quality work. I had been talking to various people and had a ballpark figure of what it would cost. This builder's price was in the ballpark. We knew his work and he could start right away so we went with him." In addition, their builder had built other homes in the same subdivision, and was familiar with local building codes and soil conditions.

The Sipeks chose the NP1348 Chesterton design from the Design America series. A contemporary design, the Chesterton features 1,890 square feet of living area neatly packaged into 1 1/2 stories. The home was built on a 1/4 acre lot. "We started looking at

Sipek Residence

plans about one year before we broke ground," says Bob. "The first plans we chose were from a company in Texas. But then we found out that the plans weren't certified for Illinois and it would've been very costly to modify them to comply." The Design America staff was able to deliver plans certified for Illinois and also incorporated some changes the Sipeks wanted to make. Among other things, they enlarged the first-floor master bath and rearranged some closet space to allow a first-floor powder room to become a third full bath. The Sipeks were somewhat pressed for time, but the Design America staff was able to meet their needs. "The company was good at rushing our changes through in about a week," says Bob.

This was Bob and Judy's first attempt at building a home for themselves, and they enjoyed the experience. Their greatest concern was finding a builder they could trust who wouldn't run into financial trouble during construction and be unable to finish. This concern wasn't great enough, however, to cause them to try their hand at being a general contractor.

The only real problem the Sipeks encountered was a time crunch towards the end of the project. There were some rain delays, and a rather complicated roofline took longer to construct than anticipated. Bob and Judy had to wait an extra six weeks to move in, but delays such as these are common. In fact, allowing enough time for construction is one piece of advice the Sipeks offer first-time home builders. They started researching plans and builders about one year in advance of construction, but really could have used a year and a half. It's also important to match the design of your home with your lifestyle. "When you pick out a floor plan, think about how you live," says Judy. "Since we don't have kids, I wanted every place I need most to be on the main floor, and the rooms that we don't use all the time somewhere else. This house fits just perfectly."

Even with the construction delays and minor problems, the Sipeks agree that building their custom home was well worth it. Neighbors are always saying how much they like the house and Bob and Judy couldn't be happier. **"It's definitely worth building yourself to get exactly what you want,"** says Judy. "We plan to retire here."

Make Design America Plans Part of Your Home-Building Experience

Many people have built their own custom homes and so can you! Allow enough research time, solicit bids from a variety of builders or subcontractors, insist on quality work, and choose Design America plans. By following these tips from successful home builders, you'll be well on your way to living in that home you've always wanted. Design America also offers books on building and construction to help you start your project with a solid foundation of knowledge. ✍

Analyze the Blueprints Before Building to Create the Best Possible Home of Your Dreams

Article by Guhner-Jahr Publishing
Build-It & Build-It Ultra

There need be nothing "stock" about a custom home built from pre-drawn mail-order plans. In fact, with imagination and/or professional guidance, thousands of homeowners have modified existing blueprints to create truly personal, character-filled homes. Changes can range from simple facade embellishments, such as articulated door and window casings, to major spatial modifications—for example, combining two small bedrooms to create a grand master suite with a bath and dressing room.

Though dramatic in effect, many custom touches may not even require new architectural drawings. Other, more substantial changes are best accomplished with the help of an architect or other design professional, who can prepare any new drawings that are needed.

In either case, it is critical to consider and decide on any changes early in the process, long before construction begins. Otherwise, any bids you solicit prior to changing the plans will be inaccurate. Worse still, if you ask for modifications during construction, your project is likely to be beset by delays and cost over-runs.

Material Choices

Among the simplest changes are those related to materials. Let's say your plans and specifications call for clapboard siding, but you prefer the more rustic look of wood shakes. Simply select the alternative material, change the specification, and you've personalized your home-to-be. Other easy-to-change materials with a potentially big impact on a home's looks include roofing and the trim around windows and doors.

One step further are changes that affect both materials and design. For example, many two-car garages are designed with a single, large door, but you may prefer the lighter look of two single-width doors. Or, instead of the double-hung windows in the plans, you may opt for the more gracious look of floor-to-ceiling casements.

In many instances it's possible to "test" the visual impact of such changes by sketching in the alternate materials on tracing paper laid over the elevations in the blueprints. These changes should not be treated lightly, however, and if you're unsure, it's a good idea to invest in some professional design help. (For more on the importance of material specifications, see "Specifying Your Dream." page 14.)

Floor Plan Changes

Another area to consider is the floor plan itself. Though today's mail-order house plans are generally well-designed with the needs of modern families in mind, it's often possible to make a change or two in the layout that turns an almost-perfect design into an ideal home for your family. Removing a single wall, for example, might create the large, open living room/dining room you desire. Or, raising the garage's walls and roof by just 4 feet could turn an unfinished storage loft into the spacious home office you need.

Kitchens and baths, which are the most complicated and most used rooms in the house, deserve special attention. A luxurious two-person shower, for example, may better suit your lifestyle than a standard tub/shower combination. Similarly, an expanded kitchen

Article Courtesy of Guhner-Jahr Publishing.

CUSTOMIZE IT !

Small changes on paper can greatly improve your plans, but make sure you decide on any modifications before construction begins.

◆ ◆ ◆

that can accommodate two sinks and dishwasher may be the perfect solution if you entertain frequently.

Again, you can begin by sketching your ideas on tracing paper laid over the blueprints. If you can't figure out the layout changes needed, seek professional advice from an architect or other design professional.

Working with Pros

If you're confident about the changes you desire but can't quite visualize or draw them, you can hire an architectural draftsperson—perhaps a local architecture student—who can turn your ideas into finished plans and/or elevations. Rates for drafting start at about $25 per hour.

If you need design help or advice about materials—especially if you're considering changes that will affect the house's structure, such as moving or removing walls—seek the services of an architect or other qualified design professional. Registered architects are trained to address both spatial and structural questions. Designers vary more in training and experience; some are best at what was traditionally called decorating, while others are fully adept at space planning.

Many architects and designers will work on an hourly consulting basis, with fees ranging from about $75 to $125 per hour or more, depending on professional accreditation, experience and location.

Kitchen and Bath Specialists

Kitchens and baths are highly specialized design areas, so make sure whatever type of design pro you choose has a lot of experience. One option is to seek out a Certified Kitchen Designer (CKD) or Certified Bath Designer (CBD). To earn this title, professionals must meet special requirements, pass tests and obtain certification from the licensing arm of the National Kitchen & Bath Association

(NKBA). In addition to providing design services, CKDs and CBDs can help you select and can provide materials and products for the kitchen and bath.

Kitchen and bath dealers, many of whom are NKBA members, work out of showrooms that sell cabinets, appliances, bath fixtures and more. Most dealers provide design services and provide products and materials.

A Custom Home Doesn't Have to be Expensive

It's true. If you're planning on building your next home, it's cheaper to customize your own design and hire your own builder than it is to choose a plan from a large developer who's building a subdivision. Even if you accept the developer's stock plans with no modifications, it will still cost you more than building a custom home from your own plans. And the home need not be large, either. No matter if your dream is for 1300 or 3000 square feet, you'll spend less by designing and building yourself.

Why it Makes Sense to Build Your Own Custom Home

You might be thinking, "But how can that be? Can't those big developers build houses cheaper because of the volume of business they do? Don't they get volume discounts on their building materials?" That might be the case, but they also incur significant costs associated with marketing their developments.

It's easy to see these marketing expenses when you take a look at a new subdivision. Consider the model homes that are built for prospective home buyers to tour. The developer has to pay for the interior designers who decorate the homes as well as for all the custom furnishings and landscaping. The salespeople who work there seven days a week must also be paid. Costly brochures promoting the subdivision must be created, and advertising space in newspapers and on television and radio must be purchased. The developer can recoup some of these expenses when the models are sold, but not all of them because the models are sold at a discount. Much of the cost gets passed on to you, the buyer, making the homes more expensive. By building yourself, using custom plans, you can avoid paying those extra costs and have a more personalized home, too!

What's the Best Source for Customized Plans?

You could hire an architect to draw up your custom plans, but you may end up spending thousands of dollars to get the design you want. A better alternative is to purchase customized plans from Design America and spend only hundreds. Design America has top-quality plans, and the expertise and the willingness to back them up with good customer service. Since we've been designing people's dreams for over 80 years, we know what you're looking for in a home. And because of the volume of our business, we can offer customized plans at prices that are 25 – 50% less than what a professional designer would charge.

Example of plan modification

Rendering courtesy of Select Home Designs   **FIG 1**

Even if your future home is less than a mansion, you'll save money by building yourself with custom plans from Design America

◆ ◆ ◆

Revised Plans after modifications   Photo courtesy of Select Home Designs

The Customization Process

The first step is to browse through our Design America Series and select the design that comes closest to your idea of a perfect home. Design America has hundreds of different designs to choose from. If the simplified drawings and renderings in our plan books give you enough information, then fax us your request for changes. Just let us know what changes you need as outlined preceeding page (pg.11, fig.1) and our architects will do the rest.

If you'd like to buy a set of plans first, Design America's helpful design staff will discuss any customization options with you at the time of your order. Feel free to ask as many questions as you like. If changes are necessary, you can tell us at the time of your order. Preferably, you should give us the modifications in writing via mail or fax so there is no confusion over any of the details.

Other home plan companies may ask you to mark up a diagram of the home with the desired changes. But NPS believes you shouldn't have to worry about drawing your plans yourself. After all, we're the architects! We'll do the sketching; you just tell us what you want changed. After we evaluate your request, we'll estimate how much the changes will cost **free** of charge and how long they will take. Of course, price and lead time will vary depending on the extent of the modifications.

NPS Can Provide Your Plans in Several Different Formats

If you won't be making any changes to the stock plans you've selected, then you should order your plans in the form of blueprints. Blueprints are non-erasable and non-reproducible so not even minor changes can be made to them by you or your builder. Order these only if you're sure nothing else will be altered. You'll probably need 4 – 7sets for everyone involved in the construction of your new home. You'll want one set for yourself, of course. The village or local government body that's responsible for approving the design will need a set. Your lender will request plans before a loan is approved, and finally, the general contractor will probably need several sets for all of the subcontractors.

If you want to make only very minor changes, ones the contractors can make themselves, then you should order plans that are reproducible. These plans can be erased and redrawn. If you only want to move a wall a few feet or enlarge a walk-in closet, these plans allow the contractor to erase lines and redraw them. Mylar, vellum plans are also reproducible, so you can make as many copies as you need for all the parties involved. Because mylar, vellum plans are reproducible, they are slightly more expensive than blueprints.

The Design America Advantage:

Other home plan companies' service will stop after you've received your modifications of the plans. They'll redraw the plans and send them off to you. But what happens if the village authorities won't approve construction because your plans don't meet local codes or ordinances? This can be a serious problem. And the fewer problems you have when building a house, the better. What good are plans for a home that can never be built? With other plan companies, you're on your own, but not with Design America.

We realize that local building codes may be complex. Our plans are drawn to meet one or more national standards. Sometimes this isn't enough, however. Regional and local authorities often have their own sets of codes that must be met. If you're building in a subdivision, the seller of the lots may impose certain building restrictions or covenants that must be followed. In some cases, you may not fully understand the codes, or some restrictions may get missed. Design America will help you wade through all of this bureaucracy and help you get your plans approved.

"We realize that the homeowner may not be well versed on the technical aspects of dealing with all of the different codes and ordinances," says David Azran, President of National Plan Service USA, Inc. "We see ourselves as being a liaison between the homeowner and the builder. If permitted, we'll actually sit down with the homeowner and builder and discuss what has to be done to get the plans approved." If your plans are questioned by village authorities because of code requirements, Design America will get in touch with the village and find out exactly which parts of the plans need clarification. Then we discuss what must be done with you and make the changes needed to earn the village's approval.

One of Design America's customers recently learned the value of this **exceptional service** when a conflict arose concerning the topography of the customer's lot. The local authorities rejected the homeowner's plans because the village felt the home's design was not compatible with a small hill on the site. The builder contended there was no hill, but the village insisted there was. After numerous discussions with the builder and the village, Design America discovered the problem. The village was using out-of-date drawings, and there really was no hill!

Peace of Mind With Your Customized Plans

We're sure you can see the value of Design America's services. This peace of mind is included in the price you pay for your customized plans. So call Design America today, at **(800) 533-4350** and let us assist you in the construction of your new home.

The More Active Your Role in Selecting Materials, Products and Techniques, the Better Your Home

Article by Guhner-Jahr Publishing
Build-It & Build-It Ultra

The best custom homes are carefully tailored to meet their owners' needs and wishes, and nowhere is this more important than in the selection of products, materials and construction techniques. After the workmen leave and you move in, the home will be a complete success only if you're pleased with the wood, glass, metal and stone used to transform your blueprints into a house.

Of course, many of the physical elements that comprise a home are spelled out in floor plans, elevations and allied documents. But some of these specifications may be generic, meaning there are still decisions to make. And even when a specific item is listed, you may prefer a different option—perhaps in-floor radiant heating rather than the forced hot-air furnace shown in the blueprints, or oak interior doors instead of pine.

Though it may seem easier to leave all these details to the contractor, the fact remains that you will live with the results, maybe for a lifetime. So the investment you make now in learning about the options will pay handsome dividends for years. Here's what to consider and how to find information and assistance.

Dollars and Sense

One of the best reasons to take an active role in product and material specification is to maintain budgetary control over your project. Obviously, the various options in each product category related to the home carry widely differing price tags, and those costs go directly to your home's bottom line.

Upgrade from plastic laminate to granite kitchen counters, for example, and your house may cost $7,500 more. Specify floor-to-ceiling ceramic tile in the baths instead of small tiled areas around the tub, and the additional cost might be $3,000 – $5,000, depending on the specific tile you choose.

Naturally, your total budget for the construction of the house will help to determine your material and product selections. The important point is to consider the many options—and their costs—early in the planning stages, ideally before putting your plans out to bid. That way the fixed price you contract for will reflect the many materials, products and techniques you want for the home, rather than choices the contractor may have made to save time and increase his profit.

If you're ready to solicit bids, but haven't made final decisions on every material, tell the contractors to exclude those elements from their prices. Or, if you have a good idea of what you're willing to spend on, say, flooring, ask them to include a flooring allowance of that dollar amount.

Rendering courtesy of Alan Mascord Design Associates

Rendering courtesy of Alan
Mascord Design Associates

Filling in the Blanks

Another key concern is to fill in the blanks on all specifications that are treated generically in your plans. Though a complete set of blueprints, materials lists and specification sheets represents a comprehensive set of instructions for building a home, it does not necessarily provide a single choice for every detail.

For example, plans may call for "hardwood flooring" without indicating the type of wood or pattern to use. Or they may indicate the size and position of appliances and plumbing fixtures, but not the brands or model numbers. The same may be true of siding, roofing, windows, heating and cooling equipment, cabinetry, door hardware, even such final details as switchplates. In the end, someone must make the decision between inexpensive knotty pine clapboard and top-quality cedar, or between brand X appliances in black versus brand Y finished in stainless steel. And, taken together, these choices will have a profound impact on what becomes your home. Rather than accept someone else's choice, consider the options available in each instance and select the one that best satisfies your needs, desires and budget.

Upgrades

Even when items are listed specifically in the plans, it's worth analyzing the choices and considering upgrades. In roofing, for example, premium asphalt shingles not only look better than standard products, but also carry 50 percent longer warranties, making them a good value over time. Energy-efficient high-performance window glazing offers similar benefits when life cycle costs are factored in, as do top-quality cabinets built to last for decades.

Other changes relate more to aesthetics, but are just as valid. If you've always wanted goldplated bath fittings, why pay for chrome-plated models? Likewise, if standard-issue oak strip flooring is not your dream for a living room, it makes little sense to pay for it now only to switch to polished maple in a few years. Want classic ceramic mosaics on the bathroom walls? Specify them now rather than remodeling later.

Construction Techniques

The techniques used by a contractor to build your home can greatly affect its quality and the amount of maintenance and repairs you'll face over the years. Though your selection of an experienced, competent builder takes care of much of this question, there are some details worth specifying if you want top quality. Here are some important ones that may or may not be listed in your existing spec sheets:

• Drywall should be affixed with screws, rather than nails, which are more likely to pop. Skim coating all ceiling and wall surfaces with joint compound produces a better looking, more plaster-like finish than simply taping the joints between drywall sheets.

• Vapor barriers should be affixed to studs and joists prior to drywall to prevent condensation in wall cavities.

• An airspace should be left between insulation and roof sheathing so that air can pass freely from eave to roof vents.

• Sills, the horizontal wood members on top of foundation walls, should be cut from pressure-treated lumber so you'll never have to worry about rot.

• Valleys, rakes and eaves—the most vulnerable parts of a roof— should have a waterproof membrane applied under flashing or shingles.

• Wood siding and exterior trim that will be painted should be back primed prior to installation; this will extend the life of a paint job.

• Interior and exterior painting should include a primer and two finish coats, which can outlast a single coat by as much as 50 percent.

Information and Assistance

The specification of products, materials and techniques is a complicated business. But the task becomes much easier if you familiarize yourself with the available options.

You should also shop local lumberyards, home centers, kitchen and bath dealers, lighting stores, etc., to see and price the possibilities. Collect manufacturers' product litera-

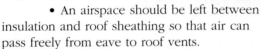

Rendering courtesy of Alan Mascord Design Associates

ture and scour design magazines for ideas as well. If it's a book you're after, we recommend "The Apple Corps Guide to the Well-Built House," by Jim Locke, Houghton Mifflin, 1988.

If you'd rather spend your money than your time, consider an architect or other design professional on a consulting basis. Working from your budget and preferences, a pro can prepare a detailed spec list for your approval, can analyze a list you've prepared and suggest worthwhile changes, or can present you with a range of good options.

However you proceed, if your aim is the best, most personal custom home possible, make sure work doesn't begin until there's a complete materials list and specification sheet that you understand and with which you're comfortable. Otherwise, you may have to start planning a remodeling soon after you move in.

✍

Financing the Construction of your Custom Home

by Kevin D. Woodard

Even before you have finalized the plans and site for your new custom home, your thoughts should turn to answering the question, "Where am I going to get the money to fund construction?" Unless you have large sums of cash saved up, you will need to take out some sort of loan to allow construction to begin. A conventional mortgage loan is not the answer at this stage, because you don't yet have a house to mortgage. For some, a home equity line of credit on their existing house can provide the cash they need. For most people wanting to build their own home, however, a *construction loan* is necessary. A permanent mortgage (also known as an *end loan* or *take-out loan*) will come later. This may sound unfamiliar to you, so let's go through the loan acquisition process one step at a time.

1. Select the source of financing

Professionals in the lending industry suggest looking to your current bank first for construction financing. You and your bank are familiar with each other, and the loan officers might already have a good idea of your present financial condition. Banks love to have multiple deposit and lending relationships with their customers and that is a good bargaining chip to have when you are negotiating the terms of your loan. But be forewarned: most banks will not lend to you if you are acting as your own general contractor unless that is how you make your living. Experience in the construction business is everything from the bank's point of view, so plan on hiring an experienced builder to oversee the construction for you unless you have a proven track record as a general contractor.

Other financial institutions can serve as funding sources as well. These include mortgage banks and brokers, and your company pension or savings plan. Retirement plans are often good for providing construction money because of the favorable terms at which you can borrow against your accumulated funds. Another source of funding is the builder himself. Your builder has a revolving line of credit with his bank and can use that to finance the construction of your new home. This arrangement simplifies things because you don't have to go to the trouble of applying for a loan at a bank. But there are disadvantages. A large deposit will be required up front and the interest the builder pays on his credit line will, of course, be passed on to you. You would pay this interest yourself anyway if you were borrowing directly from the bank, but then you would get the benefit of a tax deduction. When looking for possible sources of financing, rely on those who really know the business. Ask real estate attorneys, realtors, and local builders if they can recommend a lender.

2. Determine the type of loan that is best for you

Construction loan plus end loan. This is the most common way to finance the construction of a new home. With this arrangement, you actually get two separate loans to cover your financing needs: one for the construction phase and one for the "live in" phase after the home is built. The construction loan finances all costs associated with

Photo courtesy of Design Basics, Inc.

Photo
courtesy
of Select
Home Designs

building the house. The end loan is nothing more than a conventional mortgage that pays off the construction loan. The construction loan typically has a term of six months to a year and is an "interest only" loan. This means your monthly loan payments include only interest calculated on the amount that you have borrowed. None of your payment goes toward reducing the principal balance. The principal balance is never reduced during the entire term of the construction loan. The interest rate you pay is usually tied to the prime rate and is stated as so many points over prime. The "spread" over prime can be anywhere from 1 to 2 percentage points. The rate will fluctuate as the prime rate fluctuates and may adjust monthly or even daily. Make sure you understand exactly how and on what amount the interest is calculated.

As described below, the loan proceeds are metered out in stages. It's obviously better for the interest payments to be calculated on only that portion of the loan amount that has actually been disbursed. You don't want to pay interest on money that is not even being used yet.

Expect to pay some points when you close on your construction loan. Points are a percentage of the loan amount that must be paid up front. One point equals 1 percent. For example, a one point fee on a $100,000 loan would be $1,000. The lender charges points to cover various expenses associated with administering the loan. It's important to note that these points are not like the optional discount points you can pay on a conventional mortgage. Points on a construction loan are a pure fee for the lender and do nothing to reduce your interest rate. They typically range from 1 to 2.5 points. More points are charged on construction loans than on mortgages, because construction loans are more costly to administer. As an incentive to

stay with the same lender for your permanent mortgage, some institutions will let you use .5 point as a credit towards any points you pay on the mortgage.

A down payment will, of course, be required. Lenders usually require at least 20 percent down. This equates to a loan-to-value ratio (LTV) of 80 percent. Don't expect to get your entire loan amount disbursed to you all at once. In fact, you won't actually see any of the money at all unless you are acting as your own general contractor. The funds will be distributed to the general contractor in increments called "draws." The institution advances each draw when a specified stage of construction has been completed. For example, money will be advanced when the foundation is laid and when the framing goes up. A title company usually takes care of the actual disbursements. A representative of the lender or title company will usually inspect the project before each draw to verify that the work is being completed as planned. In addition, you the borrower may be required to sign off on each completed stage before a draw is made.

After the construction phase, when your new home is ready to be occupied, you're ready to take out the end loan. The end loan can come from the same lender as the construction loan or from a different lender.

Combination loan. Unlike the scenario presented above, in this case one loan takes care of all the financing. At the end of construction, the construction loan is simply converted into a permanent mortgage. This can save you money on closing costs since you only have to close once. Of course, you must use the same institution for construction and permanent financing.

Home equity loan. If there is a lot of equity built up in your present house, a home equity line of credit could be used as a construction loan. Equity credit lines usually have minimal paperwork and lower costs associated with them. Up to 80 percent of your home's market value may be available to use for construction financing.

3. Gather information and documents required at the time of the loan application

Here is a list of items that lenders typically require you to provide at the time you fill out a loan application:

Sworn contractor's statement. This document itemizes the contractor's estimate of all costs associated with building your home. It also lists who the subcontractors are and what they will do. It is signed by the general contractor.

General contractor's information letter. This is a form that the lender asks the builder to complete. It asks the general contractor questions about experience, insurance, bonding, etc. It helps the lender evaluate the general contractor.

Detailed blueprints and specs. The bank or other lending institution doesn't want to lend more than about 80 percent of the estimated value of the completed home. Blueprints and specs are needed for making this estimate of market value.

Signed contract between the builder and the individual. This proves you have an experienced builder working for you. It also assures the lender that the house will be built.

Deed to your lot. The lender will not grant you a loan without first knowing that you own the land on which your home will be built. If the lot is mortgaged, you will also need to have on hand all of the relevant loan documents.

Personal financial information. These are the standard items commonly required by all mortgage lenders and serve to verify your income, expenses, assets and liabilities. You'll be required to provide W-2s, paystubs, previous addresses for the past two years, name and address of employer, information on bank accounts, and outstanding loan balances, etc.

4. Close on the loan and start construction

Just as in a closing for a permanent mortgage, there are costs associated with closing on a construction loan. In addition to the points mentioned earlier, there will be recording fees, attorneys' fees, notary fees, etc. Costs such as these can vary from lender to lender, so it's a good idea to compare points and fees when shopping for a construction loan.

It's a lot of work finding construction financing and evaluating all of the options. But it will all be worth it as you watch your custom home take shape.

To help you evaluate your different financing options, Design America now offers a financing referral service. Call Design America today at **(800) 533-4350** to find out more about this new time-saving service.

Photo courtesy of
Select Home Designs

A Wealth of Information When You Decide To Build Your Own Home

Now that you've decided to build your own home and have picked the plans ...where do you go? With today's home improvement market booming, you, the consumer, have more choices then ever before. Below are some helpful hints.

LUMBER YARDS

Materials, materials, materials ..How much do I need? ...How much will they cost?...What grade of lumber should I purchase? **Your local lumber dealer is the place to start.** Here you will find a service or lumber desk. The people behind that counter just may be your next best friends. You'll typically find estimators on hand who can provide a "take off", in other words an estimate, from your blueprint or materials list. This will be based on the grade of materials that you specify. Their estimates are typically right on target. Remember that they are in the business of selling lumber. Thus you will find them both helpful and attentive because they want your business.

Although don't expect them to do it while you wait; they usually are working on numerous sets at any given time. This is especially true in early and middle spring when the majority of housing starts take place.

HOME CENTERS

Huge stores, miles of products, and helpful staffs. Although you may be overwhelmed by its sheer size you can find practically anything here. Today's typical home centers can be over 100,000 square feet with full service garden building centers. Here you get both discounted prices and idea centers. These stores have everything for home improvement and more.

You ramble past full kitchen and bath displays, order custom blinds, browse through thousands of different wall paper patterns and borders.

HARDWARE STORES

Here is the place to go when things get down to the nitty gritty or you need speed and convenience. When your stuck on a pipe fitting or need specialized fasteners your local hardware store will help you. Hardware store are the one retail outlet where a local and community atmosphere exists. Employees here will help you answer the most difficult questions and help you find the most distinguished nuts and bolts.

A Quick Guide so You'll Know What to Expect Once Construction Begin

N ow that you've settled on your plans, the joy of turning your dreams into reality begins in earnest. The wrenching matter of financing needs to be settled, and a patch of land selected. Such decisions can take weeks or even years, depending on your determination and sometimes your luck. But once the time comes to break ground, a house can't be built fast enough.

Constructing a home can take anywhere from six months to one year (or more), depending on a number of factors. The size of the house, number of workers, weather conditions and unexpected—but inevitable—delays, all make a difference. Though the order of work may vary slightly and local building inspection requirements differ, this timetable, spread over a seven-month period, will give you a sense of what to expect and when.

Rendering courtesy of
Alan Mascord Associates

Months 1 & 2

- Municipal and state permits obtained
- Site work and excavation
- Pour foundation
- Building inspection of foundation
- Frame floors
- Rough-in electrical and plumbing under floors
- Inspection of rough-in mechanical systems if house is built on slab
- Install first floor subfloor

Months 2 & 3

- Frame walls, roof and ceilings, including all door and window rough openings
- Install remaining subfloors
- Apply exterior wall and roof sheathing
- Rough-in remaining electrical and plumbing lines in wall, ceiling and floor cavities.

Months 3 & 4

- Building inspection of mechanical rough in and exposed structural work
- Apply roof flashing and shingles or other roofing material
- Install windows and exterior doors
- Apply exterior trim (window and door casings, fascia)

- Apply exterior wall finish material (i.e., clapboard, vinyl siding, stucco)

Months 5 & 6

- Install cabinets and countertops
- Apply ceramic tile in baths
- Finish plumbing and electrical work (light switches and fixtures, outlets, install sinks, tubs, etc.)
- Painting and wallpapering
- Install finish flooring

Months 6 & 7

- Install appliances
- Install hardware
- Inspection by homeowner and final touch-up work
- Site cleanup and landscaping
- Final building inspection
- Final payment to contractor
- Move in!

*Article Courtesy of
Guhner-Jahr USA Publishing*

Design America Designers

National Plan Service USA, Inc.

(The publisher of the "Design America" house plan book series)

With a history that dates back to the early 1900's, when it offered do-it-yourself plans to lumber dealers, and individual consumers, the motto of National Plan Service USA, Inc., has become "Turning Your Dreams Into Reality For Over 80 Years."

Based in Bensenville, IL, the in-house staff of registered architects and designers at NPS work to provide consumers with unlimited design possibilities. These designs range from starter homes to luxury designs, with many alternatives to fit virtually any home-building budget. Home plans from NPS can easily be modified to suit a buyer's particular needs and lifestyle. The company offers customization services, as well as general advice and assistance to make the experience of building a new home as pleasurable as possible.

Many NPS designs reflect the regional influences of the northeast and midwestern United States. These solid, time-proven designs incorporate feedback from the thousands of customers who now live in homes built from fully detailed blueprint packages provided by NPS.

DESIGN BASICS, Inc.

Design Basics, Inc. creates home plans for builders nationwide. The company markets its plans, which are designed for single family dwellings, through catalogs and trade publications. The company originated in 1983 when its primary purpose was to design plans for custom home builders in the metropolitan areas. Seeing danger in controlling too much of the local market, the company's focus shifted from designing custom home plans locally to designing plans that were adaptable anywhere. Included in these plans is a construction license allowing the purchaser to build the plan as many times as desired, and a promotional license granting the right to produce the camera-ready art work for promotional purposes. Today, Design Basics is nationally recognized through numerous awards, not only for their designs, but also for achievements in business management, corporate growth, sales, and the development of effective marketing

products. This growth and success, in turn, has helped Design Basics, Inc. define their mission statement, "Bringing People Home." All the design products and services as well as each employee are a part of a culminating effort to help people attain their dream home.

CARMICHAEL AND DAME

It was 1986 when two small-volume builders, Patrick Carmichael and Robert Dame, merged their efforts and began designing and building homes for Houston's upper-end housing market. Carmichael's forte was in finance and business management; Dame's was in translating buyers' ideas into exquisite designs. The blend of their natural talents led them to their design/build firm, Carmichael and Dame. In 1994, with more than 300 designs accumulated, Carmichael and Dame made the decision to market designs nationwide by teaming up with Design Basics, Inc. one of Americas leading home plan design firms.

Carmichael and Dame plans are nothing meticulous, averaging 20-35 pages in length with specifications as detailed as the dimension of every piece of moulding. Unlike most plan services, each of the designs have been built by its own building division, ensuring the structural soundness and buildability of each plan as a result, Carmichael and Dame is able to provide builders and consumers with both technical and construction support throughout the building process. In addition, elegant watercolor renderings are available for each of their designs, as well as a Contract Development package - a complete materials specifications and quantities reference guide. Through itsr products and designs, Carmichael and Dame hope to rekindle the passion for excellence. "One of my dreams is that the craftsman aspect of design will return to the building industry in America as it was before the turn of the century," Dame says. "Our company has tried to do that by providing designs and products with a higher level of detail, craftsmanship, architectural significance and quality."

ALAN MASCORD DESIGN ASSOCIATES, INC.

Founded in 1983, Alan Mascord Design Associates, Inc. has developed an outstanding reputation in the industry for providing innovative, buildable stock plans. Mascord first began working with local builders, providing them with great plans for their projects. Soon it became apparent that these homes could be marketed nationwide;they began a direct mail program to reach builders in other areas. This success led to publishing opportunities and soon the company's plans were being featured in several national magazines.

Always interested in providing the best possible plans available, Mascord has wholeheartedly embraced the Computer Aided Design (CAD) technology. Starting in 1986, everything Alan Mascord Design Associates, Inc. has drawn has been on CAD. This has greatly improved the quality of its drawings and the efficiency of the drafting staff. Mascord, a professional member of the A.I.B.D. and the National Association of Home Builders, has been designing homes for 25 years. "In addition to projects all over the country, many of our homes have been built in Japan by the Mitsui Company, one of the biggest builders in Japan," says Mascord.

MICHAEL E. NELSON AND ASSOCIATES, INC.

At Michael E. Nelson and Associates, Inc. creativity, craftsmanship and technology are combined to form a unique offering in the home plan industry. By utilizing computer-aided drawing technology, Michael E. Nelson and his staff produce accurate and complete designs for individuals, designers and home builders throughout the United States, producing quality designs for over ten years. Michael E. Nelson & Associates' blend of creativity and technology has brought the firm recognition through several national publications and from the American Institute of Building Designers.

A constant quest for customer satisfaction has driven Nelson and Associates to produce a portfolio of plans that meet the needs of a diverse marketplace. The vast collection of plans range from traditional to contemporary, and can be modified to suit the special needs of clients. This collection of plans brings years of experience and insight together to form an invaluable resource to home builders and individuals alike.

VAUGHN A. LAUBAN DESIGNS

Vaughn A. Lauban Designs was established in 1976 incorporating Southern traditional and Creole farmhouse styles into its designs, Vaughn A. Lauban Designs has flourished. The company's home style developed a national market with its "Back to Basics" designs. With stock plans in demand in all 50 states and several foreign countries, Vaughn A. Lauban purchased a small office building, expanded, and remodeled it to reflect this Early American feeling. "We still concentrate on the farmhouse designs, although now with additional designers on staff, Midwestern and European designs are drafted to satisfy a demanding market,"

says Vaughn A. Lauban.

SELECT HOME DESIGNS

With nearly 50 years of experience delivering top-quality and affordable residential designs to

the North American housing market, Select Home Designs is proud to continue that tradition. Since the company's inception in 1948, more than 350,000 new homes throughout North America and overseas have been built from Select Home Design plans. The Select Home Design team, however, is never content to rest on its laurels, and is constantly striving to develop the best new plans for today's lifestyles. With an outstanding collection of proven plans, virtually every architectural style and influence is represented, many featuring the latest design innovations: lavish master bathrooms, dramatic foyers, unique staircase designs, and generous use of outdoor living spaces such as decks, porches and patios. One of the most important features of a Select Home Designs plan is the flexibility it offers- which is always an important factor to consider when building a new home.

FILLMORE DESIGN GROUP

Fillmore Design Group was formed in

1960 by Robert L. Fillmore, president and founder. Over the years, the firm has grown to 12 designers and draftspeople. Fillmore designs are often characterized by their European influences, massive brick gables and high flowing, graceful roof lines". We spend considerable time on detail, particularly brick detail, and we often place a fireplace with decorative brick patterns along the front facade for focus and interest. In fact, this attention to detail extends inside the home and pays off in terms of handsome, finely wrought moulding, cornices, and other interior detailing," says Fillmore. "Each plan is done in our office by one of our experienced designers under close supervision and is checked and rechecked for accuracy before leaving the office," explains Fillmore. "Each plan is carefully thought out, down to the smallest detail by our design group. We pay attention to such items as traffic flow, open rooms with tall ceiling heights and window openings, while at the same time think of

furniture placement and wall space. We try to allow plenty of storage areas, large kitchens with good work patterns, luxurious and exciting master baths and spacious master bedrooms." Fillmore Design Group belongs to the American Institute of Building Designers and the National Association of Home Builders. The company's work has been featured in various national publications.

How To Work With An Interior Designer

The preliminaries

People hire interior designers for a variety of reasons. Some people realize that they don't have the skill or imagination to handle the job. Others don't have the time. And still others want an image - "drop-dead" chic, slick contemporary, or "instant-heritage" traditional. They hire a designer known for a particular look who can help them achieve the image they want.

A good interior designer is an interpreter who translates your *tastes* and needs into an environment that is comfortable, functional, and pleasing to look at.

The specifics

Shortly after agreeing to work with you, the designer will probably draw up a contract.

Although there is no set system of fees in the interior design business, most designers charge clients in one of several ways, or in combination:

By the hour: Some designers charge by the hour when the job is small. Others charge by the hour regardless of the scope of the job.

Flat fee: Usually arrived at based on the extent of the work and the amount of time the designer gauges it will take to complete the job.

Percentage: Some designers charge a percentage of what the total job - concept, labor, and materials - will cost, usually 20 to 30 percent, as their design fee.

Mark-up: If not charged hourly, services will be included in the retail price.

It is the designer's responsibility to come up with a plan that fits your budget. If the estimates for the job come in higher than the original budget, it's up to the designer to rework the design so that it stays in line with the amount you originally intended to spend.

Your role

Realize that the interior designer is one of the last custom professionals. The dressmaker, milliner, and bootmaker have all vanished. But the interior designer continues to produce custom one-of-a-kind design work. Custom work takes time.

You should also be aware that the interior designer is an intermediary. He or she relies on a fleet of other professionals - painters, upholsterers and specialized craftsmen - to get the job done. Foul-ups do occur. The sofa may get delayed at the upholsterer's. The painter may get backed up in his work schedule. The custom-dyed fabric that was supposed to be delicate peach could arrive in bright orange. Be prepared for setbacks.

You can sit passively by and let the designer choose everything for you. But, if you get engaged in the process, it will be much more exciting. Most designers welcome the client who shows an active interest as the transformation takes place. Working with the designer to select accent pieces, accessories, and antiques is the best way to become involved in the process, since it allows you to add your personality to the environment the professional is creating. And it's a sure way to be entirely satisfied with the final look of the room.

Carol J. Guess, ISID

Please, Help Us To Help You

In order to ensure that our Design America series best serves your needs, please assist us by filling out the questionnaire below. As a token of our appreciation, we'll send you a **FREE CATALOG** of **Project Plan Ideas**. (Please check the correct responses.)

1. Is this book your
   - ❏ 1st home plan book
   - ❏ 2nd home plan book
   - ❏ 3rd home plan book
   - ❏ _____ plan book

2. What prompted you to buy this Design America book?
   - ❏ Number of plans offered
   - ❏ Various plan styles
   - ❏ Customization
   - ❏ Looking for building ideas
   - ❏ Book category
   - ❏ Helpful articles

3. How long have you been searching for your dream home plan?
   - ❏ 0 - 6 months
   - ❏ 7 - 12 months
   - ❏ 12 - 24 months
   - ❏ More than two years

4. Would you like information on financing your dream home?
   - ❏ Yes
   - ❏ No

5. Are you looking for land to build on, if so, where?
   - ❏ Yes _____
     _____

6. When do you plan to begin construction of your new home?
   - ❏ 0 - 6 months
   - ❏ 6 - 12 months
   - ❏ Within 2 years
   - ❏ Not sure, gathering materials

7. How much do you plan to spend on materials on your new home (excluding land)?
   - ❏ Less than $100,000
   - ❏ $100,000 - $149,000
   - ❏ $150,000 - $199,000
   - ❏ More than $200,000

8. What style of home do you plan on building?
   - ❏ Traditional   ❏ Multi Family
   - ❏ Colonial   ❏ Country
   - ❏ Contemporary ❏ Vacation
   - ❏ Ranch   ❏ Victorian
   - ❏ Other _____

9. What additional information could we provide that would make it easier for you to build your dream home? (Please check all that apply)
   - ❏ Rear elevations
   - ❏ Interior elevations
   - ❏ Colored photographs of the homes
   - ❏ Approximate cost to build
   - ❏ More articles related to the home building process.
   - ❏ Other_____

10. Are you a . . . ?
    - ❏ Consumer   ❏ Building Trades
    - ❏ Professional Builder/Contractor

11. In what type of residence do you currently live?
    - ❏ Single family home   ❏ Townhouse
    - ❏ Condo / co-op   ❏ Apartment
    - ❏ Other

12. The population of the city, town you currently reside?
    - ❏ less than 20,000   ❏ 83,000-100,000
    - ❏ 21,000-41,000   ❏ 101,000- +
    - ❏ 42,000-82,000

13. What is your gross annual household income - before taxes?
    - ❏ Under $30,000
    - ❏ $31,000 - $60,000
    - ❏ $61,000 - $80,000
    - ❏ $81,000 - $100,000
    - ❏ $101,000 +

Mail or fax to: *NATIONAL PLAN SERVICE USA, INC., 222 JAMES ST., BENSENVILLE, IL 60106*

NAME _____

ADDRESS _____

CITY _____   *PLEASE FAX TO*   **1-800-344-4293**

STATE _____   ZIP _____   PHONE (_____) _____

Design America
Your Blueprints For Success

Our Blueprint Package contains nearly everything you need to get the job done properly and accurately, whether you're acting as your own general contractor or with help from an architect, designer, builder or subcontractors. Each Blueprint Package is the result of many hours of work by licensed architects or professional designers.

ACCURACY & QUALITY

Our staff of architects and professional designers have developed blueprints to ensure accuracy and quality.

VALUE

Purchase professional quality blueprints at a fraction of their development cost. With Design America, your dream home plan is attainable.

PROMPT SERVICE

Once you've chosen your dream home plan, fax your order to 1-800-344-4293 or call toll free at 1-800-533-4350. Upon receipt of your order, we will process it quickly!

SATISFACTION

With over 80 years of quality service to home plan buyers; past, present, and future, our experience and knowledge have made us a premier home plan company.

ORDER TOLL FREE
1-800-533-4350 or Fax 1-800-344-4293

After you've chosen your home plan package, simply mail or fax the accompanying order form on page 33 or call toll free on our Blueprint Hotline: 1-800-533-4350. We're ready to assist you in building your dream home.

- **HOUSE SECTIONS**
- **DETAILED FLOOR PLANS**
- **EXTERIOR ELEVATIONS**
- **INTERIOR ELEVATIONS**
- **FOUNDATION PLANS**
- **COVER SHEETS**
- **MATERIAL LIST**

Each set of blueprints is a collection of floor plans, exterior & interior elevations, details, cross-sections, diagrams and general notes showing precisely how your house is to be constructed.

Your Plans Will Show:
Cover Sheet

This artist's sketch of the exterior of the house, done in perspective, gives you an idea of how the house will look after it is built. This is only an artistic conception and may vary from actual working drawings.

Exterior Elevations

Drawn in 1/4-inch or 1/8-inch scale show the front, rear and sides of your house. General notes on exterior materials and finishes. A generic site plan may be incorporated in your blueprints.

Foundation Plan

Drawn to 1/4-inch scale, this sheet shows the complete foundation layout including support walls, excavated and unexcavated areas, if any, and foundation details. Specify slab construction, basement, or crawl when ordering.

Detailed Floor Plans

Completed in 1/4-inch scale, these plans show the layout of each floor of the house. All rooms and interior spaces are carefully dimensioned and keys are provided for cross-section details given later in the plans. The positions of all electrical outlets and switches are incorporated in this sheet.

House Sections

Large-scale cut-away views, normally drawn at 3/8-inch or 1/2-inch equals 1 foot, show sections or cut-away of the foundation, interior walls, exterior walls, floors, and roof areas. Additional cross-sections are given to show important changes in floor, ceiling or roof heights or the relationship of one level to another. Extremely valuable for construction, these sections show how the various parts of the house fit together.

Interior Elevations

These large-scale drawings show the design and placement of kitchen and bathroom cabinets, laundry areas, fireplaces, bookcases and other features. Little "extras," such as mantelpiece and wainscoting drawings, plus moulding sections, provide details that give your home that custom touch.

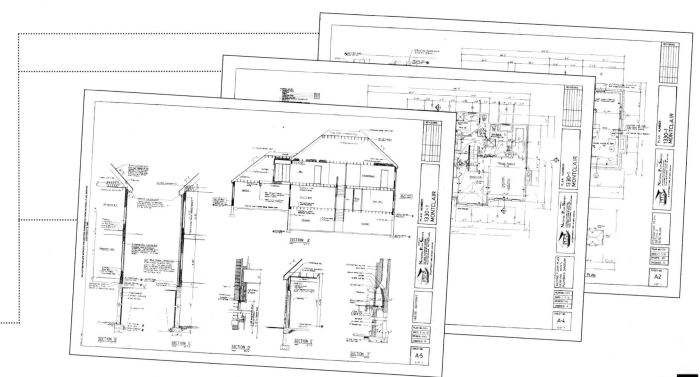

Design America Options and Services

Reversed

As Shown

Reversed Plans

Have you ever thought you've found the perfect home plan only the garage or porch is on the wrong side? The solution to this problem is in reversed, or "mirror image" plans. We can send one full set of "mirror image" plans (although the text will appear backwards) as a master guide for you and your builder.

Modifying Your Design America Home Plan

If you are considering making major changes to your design, we strongly recommend that you purchase our reproducible vellums and use the services of a professional designer, architect or ask our Design America staff. For this valuable service please call **1-800-533-4350 Architectural Dept.**

Our Reproducible Vellums and Mylars Make Modifications Easy

With a reproducible copy of our plans, a design professional can alter the drawings just the way you want. You can print as many copies of the modified plans as you need. And, since you have already started with our complete detailed plans, the cost of expensive professional services will be significantly less. Refer to the price schedule for vellums and mylars.

Don't Forget To Order Your Materials List

Our material list can help you save money. Available at a modest additional charge, the Materials List provides the quantity, dimensions, and specifications for the major materials needed to build your home. You will get faster, more accurate bids from your contractors and building suppliers. Materials Lists are available for most home plans, and can only be ordered with a set of plans. Due to differences in regional requirements and homeowner or builder preferences; electrical, plumbing and heating/ air conditioning equipment specifications are not designed specifically for each plan.

Financing Your New Home Program
Questions? Call our mortgage specialist at **1-800-533-4350**

Interior Design Services

Looking for the right image for your new home? We can help you with the right interior design image for your new home! Call our interior design expert at **1-800-533-4350**

How Many Sets Of Plans Will You Need?

Single-Set Package

We offer this set so you can study the blueprints to plan your dream home in detail. Please NOTE that the Plans in this publication are copyrighted, therefore the plans cannot be reproduced. **Ignoring Copyright laws can be a costly mistake.**

The Standard 4-Set Construction Package
- First set is for yourself.
- Second set is for your builder.
- Third set is for your village or municipality.*
- Fourth set is for your bank.

The Contractor 7-Set Construction Package
- First set is for yourself.
- Second set is for your builder.
- Third set is for your village or municipality.*
- Fourth set is for your bank.
- Fifth set is for a plumbing contractor.
- Sixth set is for a heating contractor.
- Seventh set is for additional bids.

Generic Details for the Home Builder

Because local codes and requirements vary greatly, we recommend that you obtain drawings and bids from licensed contractors to complete your mechanical plans. However, if you want to know more about techniques— and deal more confidently with subcontractors—we offer these remarkably useful detail sheets. Each is an excellent tool that will enhance your understanding of these technical subjects.

Residential Construction Details

Eight sheets feature the essentials of stick-built residential home construction. Detailed foundation options - poured concrete basement, concrete block, or monolithic concrete slab. Shows all aspects of floor, wall, and roof framing. Provides details for roof dormer, eaves, and skylights. Conforms to requirements of Uniform Building code or BOCA code.

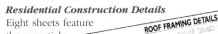

$14.95 each

Residential Plumbing Details

Nine sheets packed with information on pipe connection methods, fittings, and sizes. Shows sump pump and water softener hookups, and septic system construction. Conforms to requirements of National Plumbing Code. Color coded with a glossary of terms.   **$14.95** each

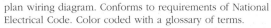

Residential Electrical Details

Nine sheets that depict all aspects of residential wiring, from simple switch wiring to the complexities of three-phase and service entrance connection. Explains service load calculations and distribution panel wiring. Shows you how to create a floor plan wiring diagram. Conforms to requirements of National Electrical Code. Color coded with a glossary of terms.

$14.95 each

Detail Plan Prices

Purchase any two (2) sets for only $22.96 or all three (3) for $29.97. See the Order Form on page 33.

Important Shipping Information

Your order is processed immediately. Allow 10 working days from our receipt of your order for normal UPS delivery. Save time with your credit card and our "800" number. UPS must have a street address or Rural Route Box number—never a post office box. Use a work address if no one is home during the day. Please call for international shipping information.

AN IMPORTANT NOTE:

1) All plans are drawn to conform to one or more of the building industry's major national building standards at the time and place they were drawn. However, due to the variety of local building regulations, your plan may need to be modified to comply with local requirements—snow loads, energy loads, seismic zones, etc. We strongly recommend that you consult with your local building officials or local architect for required information on submission of permit documents.

2) Detail plans are generic and do not conform specifically to the house plan that you purchase.

*Multiple sets of documents (blueprints) may be required by your local village or municipality building depts.

1. **Choose your Design America Plan**

2. **Would you like to customize your blueprints to your family's needs and lifestyle?**

   If YES: Talk to one of our blueprints experts at 1-800-533-4350 or in Illinois 630-238-0555

   If NO: Order the design number indicated at the top of the page, determine number of sets needed and specify if you are ordering a plan with foundation options; basement, crawl space, slab, pier.

3. **Upon having made your decision as to the design you wish to purchase, we recommend you order them through the Lumber yard, Home Center, or Hardware dealer who provided you with this book. Your local Lumber yard, Home Center, or Hardware dealer can give you valuable information and suggestions on you new dream home. Or mail, phone or fax us your blueprint order or customization request and we will process your order quickly. For accurate processing of your order please enclose check, money order, cashiers check or Master card/Visa information with the plan design number and order form (Page 33) To:**

   NPS Design America, Inc.
   Slot A-1
   P.O. Box 66973 **DA 1000**
   Chicago, Illinois 60666-0973
   Ph. 1-800-533-4350 • 630-238-0555
   Fax 1-800-344-4293 • 630-238-8885

Blueprint Prices

The cost of having an architect design a new custom home typically runs from 4 to 10 percent of the total construction cost, or from $4,000 to $10,000 for a $100,000 home. A single set of blueprints for the plans in this book ranges from $195 to $720, depending on the size of the house. Working with existing drawings may save you enough money on design fees to enable you to build a deck, upgrade your materials, or design a luxurious kitchen. Please note : garages, porches, decks, and unfinished basements are not included with the total living area, unless noted.

What will it cost to Build?

As noted in one of the articles, it is best to find out how much you can qualify for prior to building. Building cost vary widely from region to region, depending on a number of factors, including local material availability and labor costs, and the finished materials selected.

Foundation Options & Exterior Construction

Depending on your site conditions and region, your home will be built with a slab, pier, pole, crawlspace, or basement foundation. Exterior walls will be framed with either 2 by 4's or 2 by 6's, determined by structural and insulation standards in your area. Consult with your local building official in your area. Most contractors can easily adapt a home to meet the foundation and/or wall requirements for your area.

Service & Blueprint Delivery

Blueprint representatives are available to answer questions and assist you in placing your order. Plans are delivered via U.S. Mail or UPS.

Returns & Exchanges

Blueprints are specially printed and shipped to you in response to your specific order, consequently, requests for refunds cannot be honored.

Local Codes & Regulations

Because of climactic, geographic, and governmental policies set by your municipality, building codes and regulations vary from one area to another. These plans are authorized for your use only on the expressed consent that you oblige and agree to comply with all local building codes, ordinances, regulations, and requirements, including permits and inspections at time of construction.

Architectural & Engineering Seals

With increased concern about energy cost and safety, many cities and states require that an architect or engineer review and "seal" a blueprint prior to construction. To find whether this is a requirement in your area, contact your local building department.

License Agreement, Copy Restrictions & Copyright

When you purchase your blueprints, you are granted the right to use these documents to construct a single unit. All the plans in this publication are protected under the Federal Copyright Act, Title XVII of the United States Code and Chapter 37 of the Code of Federal Regulations. Each designer retains title and ownership of the original documents. The blueprints licensed to you cannot be used by or resold to any other person, copied, or reproduced by any means. The copying restrictions do not apply to reproducible blueprints. When you purchase a reproducible set of mylars or vellums, you may modify and reproduce it for your own use.

AN IMPORTANT NOTE:

1) All plans are drawn to conform to one or more of the building industry's major national building standards at the time and place they were drawn. However, due to the variety of local building regulations, your plan may need to be modified to comply with local requirements—snow loads, energy loads, seismic zones, etc. We strongly recommend that you consult with your local building officials or local architect for required information on submission of permit documents.
2) Detail plans are generic and do not conform specifically to the house plan that you purchase.

*Multiple sets of documents (blueprints) may be required by your local village or municipality building depts.

P R I C E   C O D E*

	A	B	C	D	E	F
BLUEPRINTS (Material List subject to availability)						
One Set of Blueprints	$195.00	$230.00	$275.00	$320.00	$520.00	$720.00
Four Sets of Blueprints	$265.00	$310.00	$355.00	$400.00	$1,020.00	$1,220.00
Seven Sets of Blueprints	$320.00	$360.00	$405.00	$450.00	$1,420.00	$1,620.00
Reproducible Vellum (1 Set)	$480.00	$540.00	$600.00	$675.00	$1,645.00	$1,845.00
Reproducible Mylar (1Set)	$500.00	$560.00	$620.00	$695.00	$1,665.00	$1,865.00
Additional regular sets	$40.00	$40.00	$40.00	$40.00	$180.00	$180.00
Mirror reverse	$40.00	$40.00	$40.00	$40.00	$180.00	$180.00
SHIPPING AND HANDLING 1–7 sets						
Regular U.S.(6-10 days)	$10.00	$13.00	$16.00	$19.00	$22.00	$25.00
Express (2-3 days)	$25.00	$28.00	$31.00	$34.00	$37.00	$40.00
Overnight*	$30.00	$33.00	$36.00	$39.00	$42.00	$45.00
Other**	Call	Call	Call	Call	Call	Call
*Not available on certain plans **For delivery outside U.S.						
MATERIAL LIST *Material list subject to availability						
1-3 copies	$40.00	$40.00	$40.00	$40.00	CALL	CALL
4-7 copies	$45.00	$45.00	$45.00	$45.00	CALL	CALL
PREVIEW PLANS (11" X 17" format)						
1 ea. B/W format*	$15.00	$15.00	$15.00	$15.00	CALL	CALL
1 ea. Colored format*	$40.00	$40.00	$40.00	$40.00	CALL	CALL
*Subject to availability						
DESIGN SHEETS (8.5" X 11" format)						
1 ea. B/W sell sheets*	$25.00	$25.00	$25.00	$25.00	—	—
100 qty. ea. B/W sell sheets*	$38.00	$38.00	$38.00	$38.00	—	—
200 qty. ea. B/W sell sheets*	$58.00	$58.00	$58.00	$58.00	—	—
ARCHITECTURAL RENDERING OF HOME						
B/W 8"X10" PMT Format*	$89.00	$89.00	$89.00	$89.00	CALL	CALL
Colored 8"X10" PMT format*	$115.00	$115.00	$115.00	$115.00	CALL	CALL

*Subject to availability

Step 1.

BLUEPRINTS ORDER FORM

Step 3.

PURCHASED BOOK FROM: _____ TOWN: _____

DATE BOOK WAS PURCHASED: _____

NAME: _____

ADDRESS: _____

CITY: _____ STATE: _____ ZIP: _____

PHONE #: ( ) _____

Enclosed is: ❑Check   ❑Money Order   CARD NUMBER: _____

Bill: ❑Visa   ❑Master Card   EXPIRATION DATE MONTH/YEAR_____/_____

Checks Payable to: NPS Design America, Inc.

SIGNATURE _____

Step 2.

Plan Number _____ Price Code_____

Foundation Type:_____
(Many plans offer different options; others are designed to one type of condition).

Number of Sets: ____One Set   ____Four Sets   ____Seven Sets   ____Vellum   ____Mylar

Additional Sets: _____ Qty. ($40.00 Price Code A-D; Price Code E-F Call) Prices good for 60 days

Mirror Reverse:_____ ($40.00)

Material List: _____(See List)

Preview Plan Number: _____ (See List)

Design Sheets: ____1ea. ____100 qty. ____200 qty. of Plan Number:_____
(Check appropriate space)

Architectural Rendering: ____B/W ____Colored (See List) Plan Number:_____

Send Your Order To: NPS Design America, Inc.
Slot A-1 P.O. Box 66973 Dept. DA1000, Chicago, IL, 60666-0973

Order Toll Free 1-800-533-4350 Or 24-Hour Fax Ordering 1-800-344-4293

Detail Plans

_____**H801C Construction**
@ $14.95 each
_____**H802E Electrical**
@ $14.95 each
_____**H803P Plumbing**
@ $14.95 each
Any two (2) - $22.96
Any three (3) - $29.97

Write in dollar figure

$_____Detail plans

$_____Blueprints

$_____Material List

$_____Preview Plans

$_____Design Sheets

$_____Arch Rendering

$_____Shipping & Handling

$_____Sub Total

$_____Sales Tax (IL 6.75%)

$_____**Total**

33

*Prices may change without notice

34

22'-0"

26'-6"

F.

W.H.

BATH

BEDROOM
9'-6" x 10'-0"

R.

KITCHEN
9'-0" x 7'-6"

WOOD STOVE

LIVING ROOM
12'-4" x 11'-0"

NOOK
9'-0" x 7'-0"

Total Living Area   527 sq. ft.

PRICE CODE: A

PLAN NPSTIL

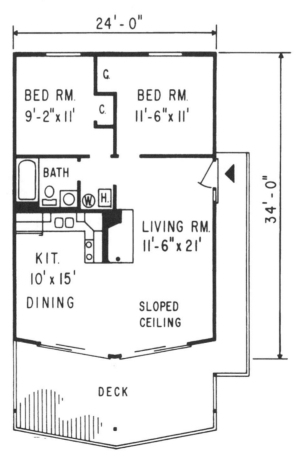

24'- 0"

BED RM.
9'-2" x 11'

C.

C.

BED RM.
11'-6" x 11'

34'- 0"

BATH

W H.

LIVING RM.
11'-6" x 21'

KIT.
10' x 15'

DINING

SLOPED
CEILING

DECK

Total Living Area   792 sq. ft.

PRICE CODE: A

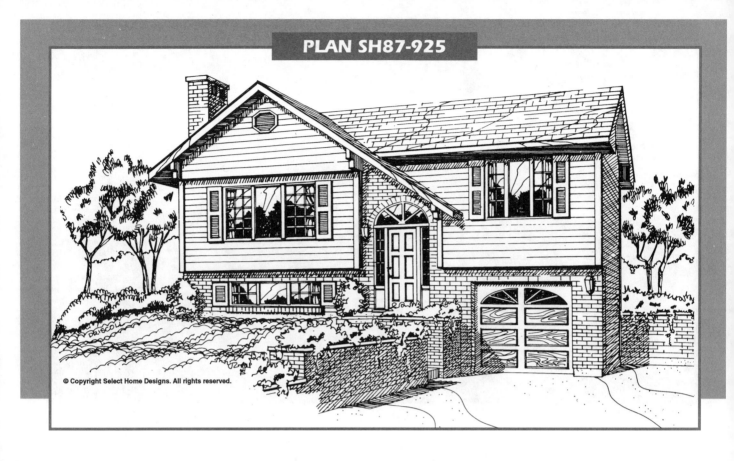

36

Plans include all exteriors shown

WORKSHOP

W D

F

9'3 x 14'7 br 4

Alternative Lower Level

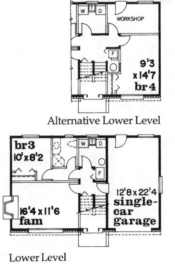

br3 10'x8'2

W T D

F

12'8 x 22'4 single-car garage

16'4 x 11'6 fam

Lower Level

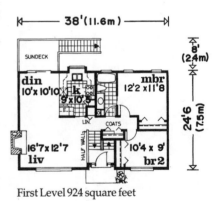

38' (11.6m)

8' (2.4m)

SUNDECK

din 10'x 10'10

k 9'x 10'5

mbr 12'2 x11'8

LIN

COATS

24'6 (7.5m)

HALF WALL

16'7x 12'7 liv

10'4 x 9' br2

First Level 924 square feet

Features

- Two-bedroom design has room for expansion
- Plans come with a choice of two elevations, one with a single-car garage.
- Living room overlooks the cathedral entry.
- Efficient U-plan shaped kitchen conveniently serves the dining room.
- Boxed-out kitchen window rests over the sink.
- Design may be built with or without a garage.

- With the garage, the unfinished lower level offers 646 square feet for future development; without the garage, 736 square feet.
- Suggested lower level layout includes a family room, two additional bedrooms, workshop plan and bathroom.

Lower Level	646 sq. ft.
First Level	924 sq. ft.
Total Living Area:	1570 sq. ft.

PRICE CODE: B

CUSTOMIZE IT!

ORDER TOLL FREE 1▪800▪533▪4350 24-HOUR FAX ORDERING 1▪800▪344▪4293

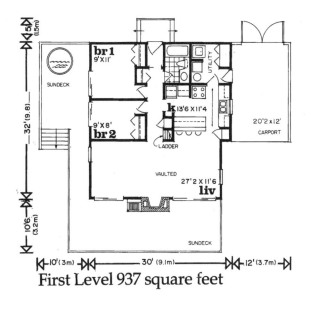

First Level 937 square feet

br 1
9'X11'

SUNDECK

br 2
9'X8'

LADDER

UTILITY

k 13'6 X11'4

20'2 x12'
CARPORT

VAULTED

27'2 X11'6
liv

SUNDECK

5' (1.5m)
32' (9.8)
10'6 (3.2m)

10'(3m) — 30' (9.1m) — 12' (3.7m)

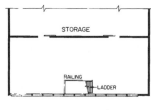

STORAGE

RAILING
LADDER

Second Level

Features

- Space-efficient leisure home offers many extras.
- Optional carport will add an additional 12 feet to the width of the home.
- Sundeck, with built-in barbecue and hot tub, invites outdoor entertaining.
- Living room boasts soaring vaulted ceiling, large fireplace and sliding glass doors to sundeck.
- Galley-style kitchen conveniently services breakfast bar and dining area.
- Bedrooms have easy access to sundeck.

Total Living Area   **937 sq. ft.**

PRICE CODE: A

PLAN NPARR

38

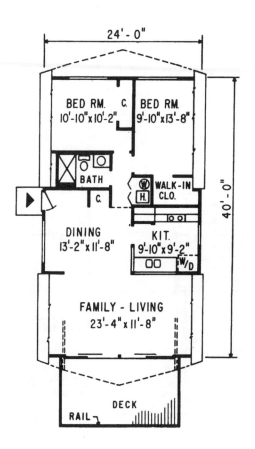

24' - 0"

40' - 0"

BED RM. 10'-10"x10'-2" C.

BED RM. 9'-10"x13'-8"

BATH

C.

WALK-IN CLO.

DINING 13'-2"x11'-8"

KIT. 9'-10"x9'-2"

W/D

FAMILY - LIVING 23'-4"x11'-8"

DECK

RAIL

Total Living Area   **960 sq. ft.**

PRICE CODE: A

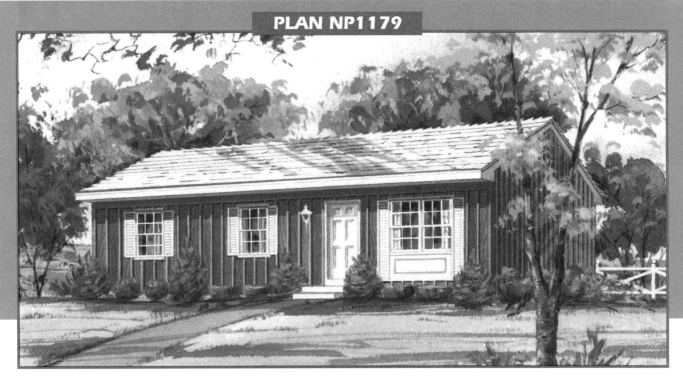

PLAN NP1179

40'-0"

24'-0"

storage

BEDROOM
11'-3" x 11'-3"

w d

FAMILY-KITCHEN
16'-8" x 11'-2"

B

L h W C

C

C

BEDROOM
11'-3" x 9'-4"

C
C

BEDROOM
9'-7" x 8'-4"

LIVING ROOM
15'-3" x 12'-8"

PLAN 2 WITHOUT BASEMENT

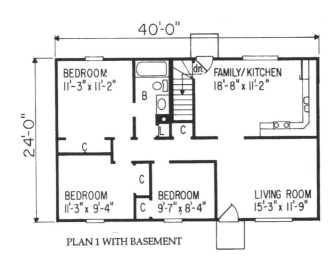

40'-0"

24'-0"

BEDROOM
11'-3" x 11'-2"

dn

FAMILY/KITCHEN
18'-8" x 11'-2"

B

L C

C

BEDROOM
11'-3" x 9'-4"

C
C

BEDROOM
9'-7" x 8'-4"

LIVING ROOM
15'-3" x 11'-9"

PLAN 1 WITH BASEMENT

Pioneer

Features

• Small home packs a lot of space into a tight floor plan.

• Entry into living room with L-shaped kitchen and dining area at rear of home.

• One centrally located full bath serves three bedrooms in left wing.

39

Total Living Area   **960 sq. ft.**

PRICE CODE: A

PLAN NP1178

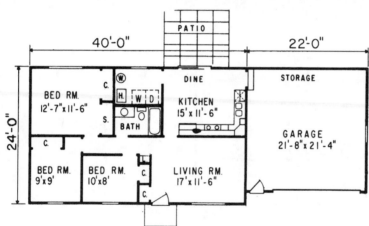

PLAN 2 WITHOUT BASEMENT

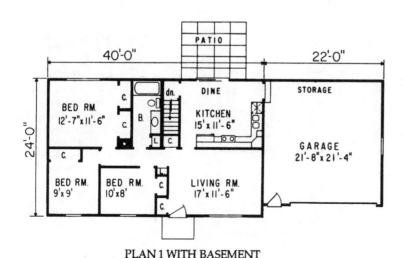

PLAN 1 WITH BASEMENT

Gabled Ranch

Features

- Small, reverse gable design saves money through simplicity of design.
- Enter directly into small living room area with L-shaped kitchen and dining area.
- Sliding glass doors at rear lead out to patio.
- Three bedrooms are served by one full bath.

Total Living Area   **960 sq. ft.**

PRICE CODE: A

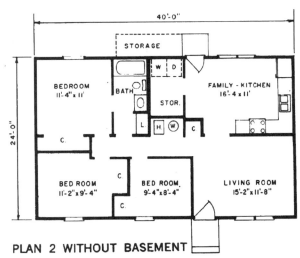

PLAN 2 WITHOUT BASEMENT

STORAGE

BEDROOM
11'-4" x 11'

BATH

W D

FAMILY - KITCHEN
16'-4 x 11'

STOR.

C.

BED ROOM
11'-2"x 9'-4"

C.

BED ROOM
9'-4"x 8'-4"

LIVING ROOM
15'-2"x 11'-8"

40'-0"

24'-0"

41

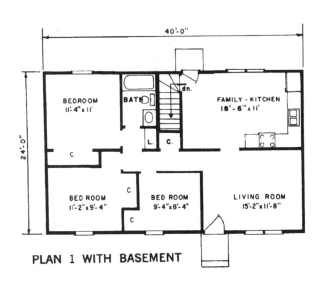

PLAN 1 WITH BASEMENT

BEDROOM
11'-4" x 11'

BATH

FAMILY - KITCHEN
18'-6" x 11'

C.

BED ROOM
11'-2"x 9'-4"

C.

BED ROOM
9'-4"x 8'-4"

LIVING ROOM
15'-2"x 11'-8"

40'-0"

24'-0"

Features

- This small Colonial starter home is the perfect choice for a family that must follow a tight budget.
- Economical construction costs are assured by the straightforward floor plan and truss roof construction.
- Energy-saving features will reduce your energy cost for years to come.
- Three bedroom and a single bath occupy one wing while the opposite wing contains the L-shaped kitchen and the family/living room.

Total Living Area   **960 sq. ft.**

PRICE CODE: A

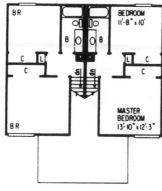

SECOND FLOOR

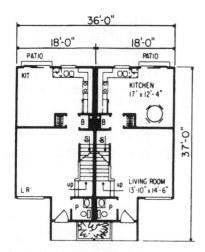

FIRST FLOOR PLAN 1 WITH BASEMENT

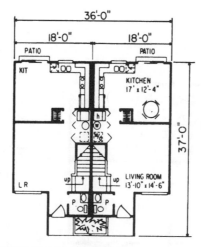

FIRST FLOOR PLAN WITHOUT BASEMENT

Dynamic Duplex

Features

- Flexible duplex unit can be grouped together as townhouses.
- Small size with maximum living space.
- Attractive entrance provides shelter from the elements.
- Each unit contains first-floor living room with powder room and country kitchen with dining area.
- Second floor contains two large bedrooms with full bath.

First Floor	554 sq. ft.
Second Floor	469 sq. ft.
Total Living Area	1,023 sq. ft.

PRICE CODE: A

PLAN NP1181

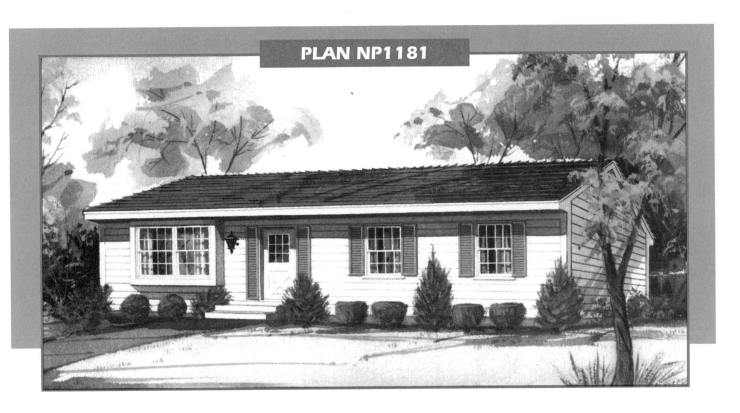

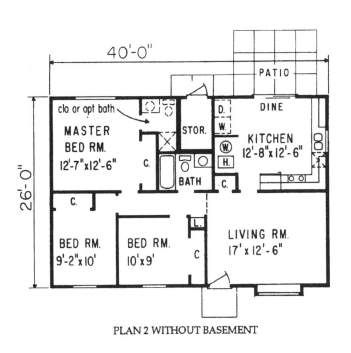

40'-0"

26'-0"

PATIO

clo. or opt bath

MASTER BED RM.
12'-7"x12'-6"

STOR.

D.

W.

DINE

KITCHEN
12'-8"x12'-6"

W.

H.

c.

BATH

c.

c.

BED RM.
9'-2"x10'

BED RM.
10'x9'

L.

C

LIVING RM.
17'x 12'-6"

PLAN 2 WITHOUT BASEMENT

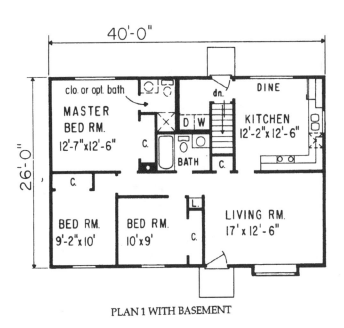

40'-0"

26'-0"

clo. or opt. bath

MASTER BED RM.
12'-7"x12'-6"

dn.

D   W

DINE

KITCHEN
12'-2"x12'-6"

c.

BATH

c.

c.

BED RM.
9'-2"x10'

BED RM.
10'x9'

L.

c.

LIVING RM.
17'x 12'-6"

PLAN 1 WITH BASEMENT

Total Living Area   **1,040 sq. ft.**

PRICE CODE: A

CUSTOMIZE IT!

ORDER TOLL FREE   **1 ▪ 800 ▪ 533 ▪ 4350**   **24-HOUR FAX ORDERING**   **1 ▪ 800 ▪ 344 ▪ 4293**

PLAN NP1186

MAIN LEVEL

DINING
9'-8" x 12'

KITCHEN
11' x 11'-9"

BED ROOM
10' x 11'-9"

B.

L.

S.

C.

C.

LIVING ROOM
18'-2" x 13'-2"

C.

up

dn.

rail

MASTER BED RM.
14'-4" x 10'-9"

dn.

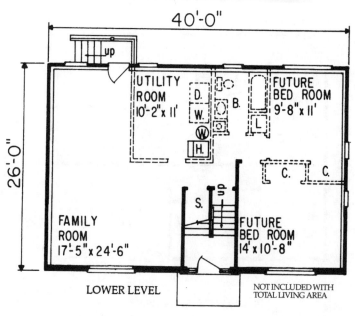

LOWER LEVEL

40'-0"

26'-0"

up

UTILITY ROOM
10'-2" x 11'

D.

W.

W

H.

B.

FUTURE BED ROOM
9'-8" x 11'

L.

C.

C.

FAMILY ROOM
17'-5" x 24'-6"

S.

up

FUTURE BED ROOM
14' x 10'-8"

NOT INCLUDED WITH
TOTAL LIVING AREA

44

Main Level	1,040 sq. ft.
Total Living Area	1,040 sq. ft.

PRICE CODE: A

PLAN NP HARBOR POINT

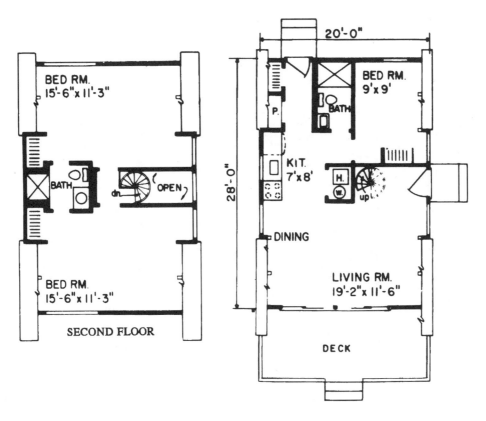

SECOND FLOOR

BED RM.
15'-6" x 11'-3"

BATH

dn OPEN

BED RM.
15'-6" x 11'-3"

20'-0"

BED RM.
9' x 9'

P.

BATH

KIT.
7' x 8'

28'-0"

H.
W. upl

DINING

LIVING RM.
19'-2" x 11'-6"

DECK

First Floor	560 sq. ft.
Second Floor	490 sq. ft.
Total Living Area	1,050 sq. ft.

PRICE CODE: A

CUSTOMIZE IT!

ORDER TOLL FREE 1■800■533■4350   24-HOUR FAX ORDERING 1■800■344■4293

PLAN NPLOD

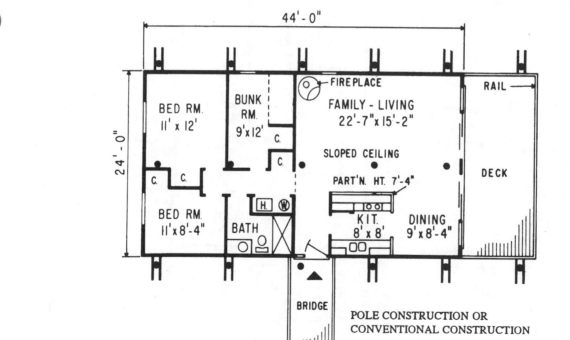

44' - 0"

24' - 0"

BED RM.
11' x 12'

BUNK
RM.
9'x12'

C.

FIREPLACE

FAMILY - LIVING
22'-7"x 15'-2"

SLOPED CEILING

PART'N. HT. 7'-4"

RAIL

DECK

C.

C.

C.

C.

BED RM.
11'x 8'-4"

BATH

H.

W.

KIT.
8'x 8'

DINING
9'x 8'-4"

BRIDGE

POLE CONSTRUCTION OR
CONVENTIONAL CONSTRUCTION

46

Total Living Area   1,056 sq. ft.

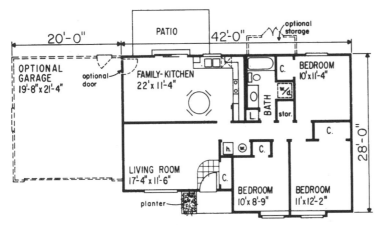

PLAN 2 WITHOUT BASEMENT

- 20'-0" — OPTIONAL GARAGE 19'-8" x 21'-4"
- optional door
- PATIO
- 42'-0"
- optional storage
- FAMILY- KITCHEN 22' x 11'-4"
- BEDROOM 10' x 11'-4"
- C.
- BATH
- stor.
- L
- h. w. C.
- C.
- LIVING ROOM 17'-4" x 11'-6"
- C.
- planter
- BEDROOM 10' x 8'-9"
- BEDROOM 11' x 12'-2"
- 28'-0"

47

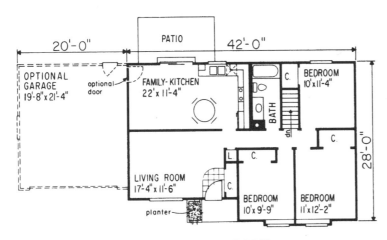

PLAN 1 WITH BASEMENT

- 20'-0"
- OPTIONAL GARAGE 19'-8" x 21'-4"
- optional door
- PATIO
- 42'-0"
- FAMILY- KITCHEN 22' x 11'-4"
- BEDROOM 10' x 11'-4"
- C.
- BATH
- C.
- LIVING ROOM 17'-4" x 11'-6"
- L
- C.
- C.
- planter
- BEDROOM 10' x 9'-9"
- BEDROOM 11' x 12'-2"
- 28'-0"

Venture

Features

- Well designed floor plan makes the best use of space.
- Exterior of entryway graces with built-in planter.
- L-shaped kitchen and adjacent dining/family room located at rear of home.
- Sleeping quarters include three bedrooms and one full bath.
- Optional garage can be added.

Total Living Area	1,096 sq. ft.

PRICE CODE: A

CUSTOMIZE IT!

ORDER TOLL FREE 1•800•533•4350   24-HOUR FAX ORDERING 1•800•344•4293

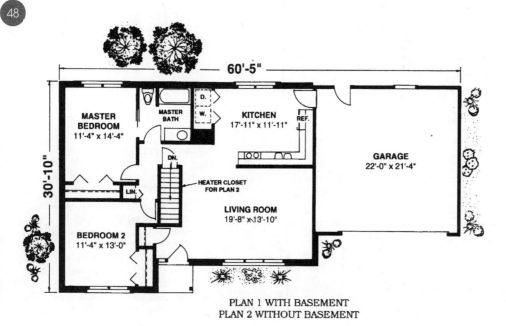

60'-5"

30'-10"

MASTER
BEDROOM
11'-4" x 14'-4"

MASTER
BATH

D.

W.

KITCHEN
17'-11" x 11'-11"

REF.

GARAGE
22'-0" x 21'-4"

DN.

HEATER CLOSET
FOR PLAN 2

LIN.

LIVING ROOM
19'-8" x 13'-10"

BEDROOM 2
11'-4" x 13'-0"

PLAN 1 WITH BASEMENT
PLAN 2 WITHOUT BASEMENT

Basic Serenity

Features

- Compact construction for easy living marks this design.
- Entryway leads to large living room.
- Garage entrance to kitchen.
- L-shaped kitchen work area with laundry facilities tucked away to the left and rear access to back yard.
- Master bedroom and second bedroom share full bath.

Total Living Area   1,102 sq. ft.

PRICE CODE: A

PLAN NP1194

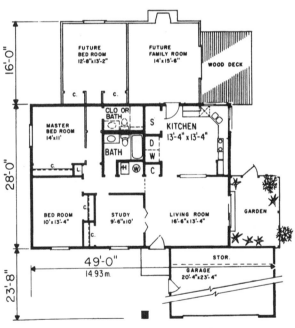

PLAN 2 WITHOUT BASEMENT

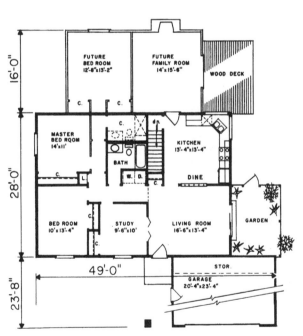

PLAN 1 WITH BASEMENT

49

Outlander

Features

- This rustic Colonial design is the ideal starter home for the economy-minded home builder.
- Attached single-car port with enclosed storage is perfect for milder climates.
- Enclosed porch leads directly into the living room.
- Combined kitchen/family room occupies rear of home.

- Three bedrooms share a full bath, with second bath optional.
- Future addition of bedroom and family room, 448 square feet.

Total Living Area   **1,120 sq. ft.**

PRICE CODE: A

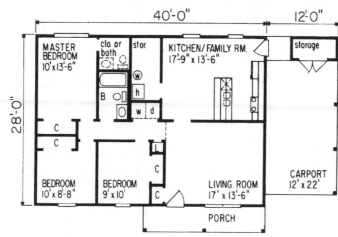

40'-0"   12'-0"

MASTER BEDROOM 10' x 13'-6"

clo. or bath   stor.

KITCHEN/FAMILY RM. 17'-9" x 13'-6"

storage

B.

28'-0"

C
C

BEDROOM 10' x 8'-8"

BEDROOM 9' x 10'

C
C

LIVING ROOM 17' x 13'-6"

CARPORT 12' x 22'

PORCH

PLAN 2 WITHOUT BASEMENT

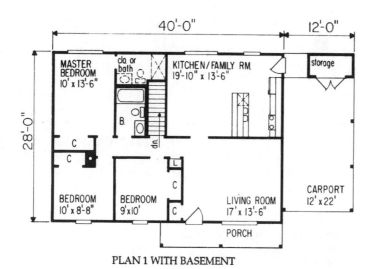

40'-0"   12'-0"

MASTER BEDROOM 10' x 13'-6"

clo. or bath

KITCHEN/FAMILY RM. 19'-10" x 13'-6"

storage

B.

28'-0"

C
C

BEDROOM 10' x 8'-8"

BEDROOM 9' x 10'

C
C

LIVING ROOM 17' x 13'-6"

CARPORT 12' x 22'

PORCH

PLAN 1 WITH BASEMENT

Palisades

Features

- Rustic, colonial design is perfect starter home for those with economy in mind.
- Single-car, attached carport is ideal for milder climates.
- Enclosed porch leads directly into the living room.
- Combined kitchen and family room occupies rear of home.
- Three bedrooms share one full bath, with option of adding second bath.

Total Living Area   1,120 sq. ft.

PRICE CODE: A

PLAN NP1193

51

PLAN 2 WITHOUT BASEMENT

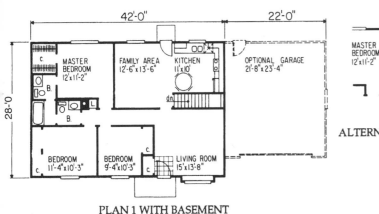

PLAN 1 WITH BASEMENT

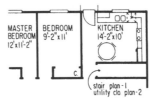

ALTERNATE 4th BEDROOM PLAN

Energy Efficient Ranch

Features

- Efficient living spaces, optimal comfort.
- Two bedrooms share a double-lavatory bathroom with the master bedroom for optimal use of space.
- A large family area adjoins the kitchen with eating area.
- The entryway opens to a living room with bow window.
- An alternate fourth bedroom plan is available in place of the family room.

Total Living Area	1,176 sq. ft.

PRICE CODE: A

52

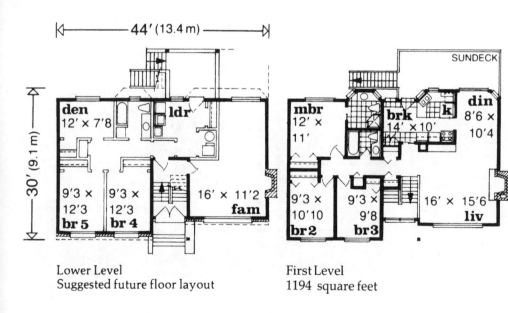

44' (13.4 m)

30' (9.1 m)

| den | ldr |
| 12' × 7'8 | |

| 9'3 × 12'3 | 9'3 × 12'3 | 16' × 11'2 |
| **br 5** | **br 4** | **fam** |

Lower Level
Suggested future floor layout

SUNDECK

mbr	brk	din
12' × 11'	14' × 10'	8'6 × 10'4
		k

| 9'3 × 10'10 | 9'3 × 9'8 | 16' × 15'6 |
| **br 2** | **br3** | **liv** |

First Level
1194 square feet

Features

- The double doors with a circlehead transom over create a grand entry to this compact three-bedroom home.
- Economical to build, this design provides many extras.
- Railing separates the living room from the vaulted entry below.
- Country-style kitchen efficiently serves the reakfast and dining areas.
- Master bedroom features an ensuite bay with shower.
- Lower level offers 522 square feet for future development.
- Suggested layout includes a family room, laundry facilities and rough-in plumbing for a bathroom.

Total Living Area   1,194 sq. ft.

PRICE CODE: A

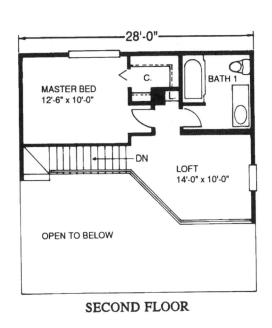

MASTER BED
12'-6" x 10'-0"

BATH 1

C.

L.

DN

LOFT
14'-0" x 10'-0"

OPEN TO BELOW

28'-0"

SECOND FLOOR

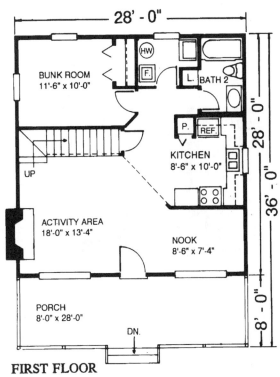

28' - 0"

BUNK ROOM
11'-6" x 10'-0"

HW

F.

L.

BATH 2

P.

REF.

KITCHEN
8'-6" x 10'-0"

UP

ACTIVITY AREA
18'-0" x 13'-4"

NOOK
8'-6" x 7'-4"

PORCH
8'-0" x 28'-0"

DN.

28' - 0"

36' - 0"

8' - 0"

FIRST FLOOR

First Floor	784 sq. ft.
Second Floor	416 sq. ft.
Total Living Area	1,200 sq. ft.

PRICE CODE: A

PLAN NP ASPEN

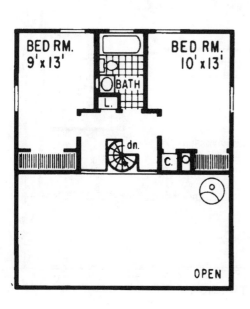

SECOND FLOOR

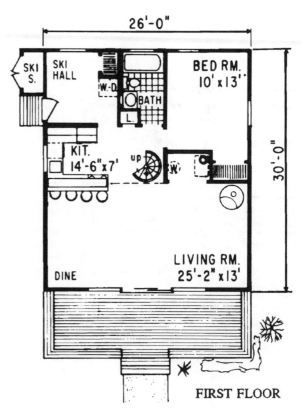

FIRST FLOOR

First Floor		780 sq. ft.
Second Floor		429 sq. ft.
Total Living Area		1,209 sq. ft.

PRICE CODE: A

54

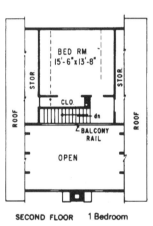

SECOND FLOOR   1 Bedroom

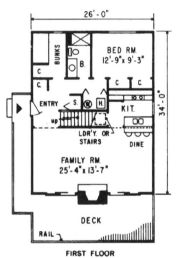

FIRST FLOOR

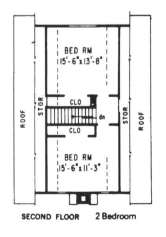

SECOND FLOOR   2 Bedroom

Cross Section
1 BED RM.

Plan with 3 Bedroom

First Floor	884 sq. ft.
Second Floor	550 sq. ft.
Total Living Area	1,434 sq. ft.

Plan with 2 Bedroom

First Floor	884 sq. ft.
Second Floor	327 sq. ft.
Total Living Area	1,211 sq. ft.

PRICE CODE: A

CUSTOMIZE IT!

ORDER TOLL FREE   1▪800▪533▪4350   24-HOUR FAX ORDERING   1▪800▪344▪4293

PLAN NPJUN

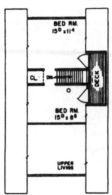

LOFT AREA
DESIGN A or B

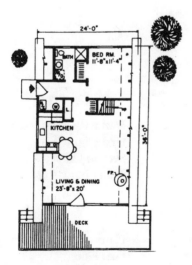

FIRST FLOOR
DESIGN B

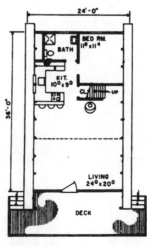

FIRST FLOOR
DESIGN A

First Floor	864 sq. ft.
Second Floor	360 sq. ft.
Total Living Area	1,224 sq. ft.

PRICE CODE: A

56

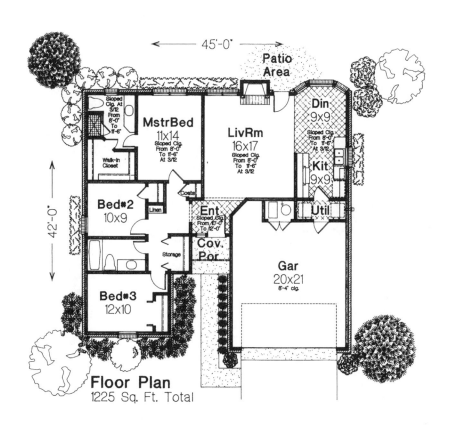

45'-0"

42'-0"

Patio Area

MstrBed 11x14
Sloped Clg. From 8'-0" To 11'-6" At 3/12

LivRm 16x17
Sloped Clg. From 8'-0" To 11'-6" At 3/12

Din 9x9
Sloped Clg. From 8'-0" To 11'-6" At 3/12

Kit 9x9

Walk-in Closet

Bed#2 10x9

Linen

Coats

Ent
Sloped Clg. From 11'-0" To 12'-0"

Util

Storage

Cov. Por

Bed#3 12x10

Gar 20x21
8'-4" clg.

Floor Plan
1225 Sq. Ft. Total

57

Total Living Area	1,225 sq. ft.

CUSTOMIZE IT!

ORDER TOLL FREE 1■800■533■4350   24-HOUR FAX ORDERING 1■800■344■4293

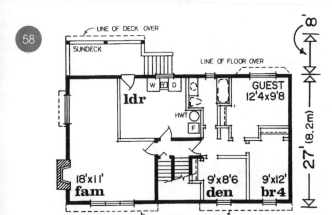

Lower Level

(OPTIONAL LAYOUT)

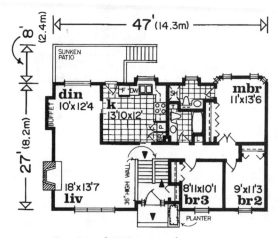

First Level 1282 square feet

Features

- Bold horizontal siding and clean lines create a pleasing exterior for this compact home.
- Unfinished lower level provides 1122 square feet for future development.
- Living/dining room flow together, creating a spacious living area. Country kitchen is an ideal gathering place for the whole family.
- Skylit country kitchen has room for a breakfast table.
- Master bedroom, tucked in windowed bay, has three-piece ensuite. Suggested lower level includes two additional bedrooms, den and large family room – an ideal in-law suite.

Total Living Area: 1,282 sq. ft.

PRICE CODE: A

PLAN NP KINGSPORT

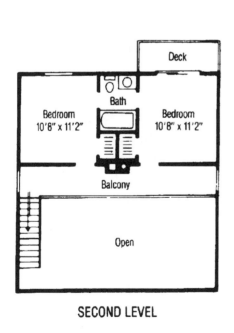

Deck

Bath

Bedroom
10'8" x 11'2"

Bedroom
10'8" x 11'2"

Balcony

Open

SECOND LEVEL

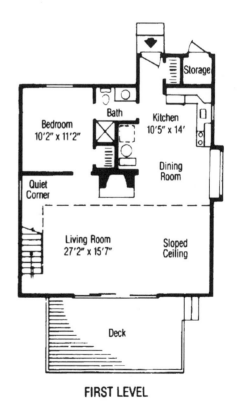

Storage

Bath

Kitchen
10'5" x 14'

Bedroom
10'2" x 11'2"

Dining Room

Quiet Corner

Living Room
27'2" x 15'7"

Sloped Ceiling

Deck

FIRST LEVEL

First Floor	811 sq. ft.
Second Floor	488 sq. ft.
Total Living Area	1,299 sq. ft.

PRICE CODE: A

CUSTOMIZE IT!

ORDER TOLL FREE 1■800■533■4350   **24-HOUR FAX ORDERING** 1■800■344■4293

Lower Level

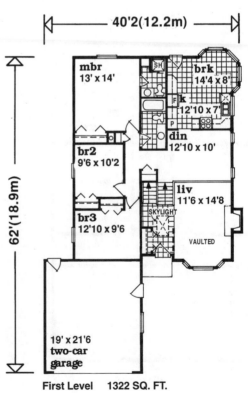

40'2(12.2m)

62'(18.9m)

First Level   1322 SQ. FT.

Features

- Handsome starter or retirement home with added features.
- Vaulted living room, with fireplace and bay window, shares one level with the skylit foyer.
- Railed dining room overlooks the living room.

- Efficient kitchen has a breakfast carousel and access to rear yard.
- Master bedroom has private ensuite with shower.

Total Living Area:·   **1,322 sq. ft.**

PRICE CODE: B

PLAN SH75-1343

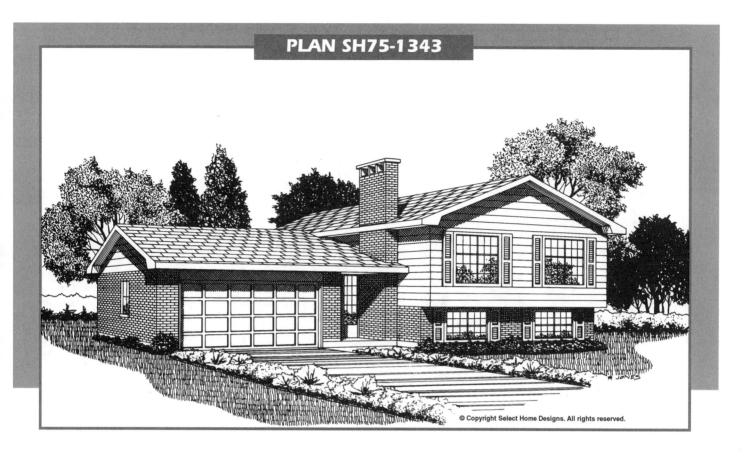

61

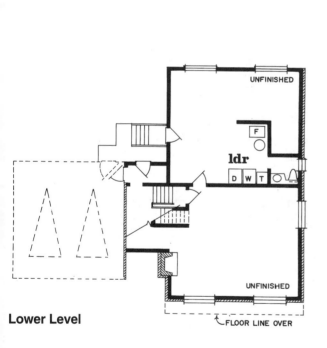

Lower Level

FLOOR LINE OVER

UNFINISHED

ldr

D W T

F

UNFINISHED

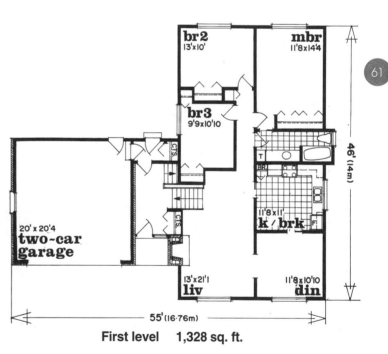

br2
13'x10'

mbr
11'8x14'4

br3
9'9x10'10

k / brk
11'8x11'

liv
13'x21'1

din
11'8x10'10

two~car garage
20' x 20'4

46' (14m)

55' (16·76m)

First level   1,328 sq. ft.

Features

- Weather-protected entry.
- Stepping up from the foyer is a spacious living room.
- Country kitchen serves the breakfast area and dining room.
- Landing steps down to a unfinished lower level, which offers 1098 square feet for future development.
- Potential for a family room or in-law suite in the lower level.
- Ample natural light spills into the lower level.

Total Living Area   1,328 sq. ft.

PRICE CODE: B

CUSTOMIZE IT!

ORDER TOLL FREE   1▪800▪533▪4350   24-HOUR FAX ORDERING   1▪800▪344▪4293

PLAN SH90-1381

42' (12.8m)

62

BASEMENT STAIR LOCATION

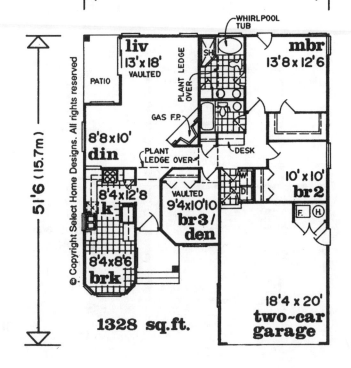

51'6 (15.7m)

liv 13'x 18' VAULTED

PATIO

PLANT LEDGE OVER

WHIRLPOOL TUB

SH

mbr 13'8 x 12'6

GAS F.P.

PLANT LEDGE OVER

DESK

8'8 x 10' **din**

PLANT LEDGE OVER

VAULTED 9'4 x 10'10 **br3/ den**

8'4 x 12'8 **k**

10' x 10' **br 2**

F. H

8'4 x 8'6 **brk**

1328 sq.ft.

18'4 x 20' **two~car garage**

Features

- Designed to capture the view to the rear of the lot.
- Home may be finished in California stucco or horizontal siding.
- Kitchen, with abundant counter space and pass through to the dining room, adjoins the breakfast bay.
- Plant ledge over the entry adorns the dining room.

- Living room features corner positioned fireplace and sliding glass door to the garden patio.
- Clerestory window brightens third bedroom or den.
- Master bedroom boasts a walk-in closet, French door to the garden and ensuite with twin vanity and spa.

Total Living Area: 1,328 sq. ft.

PRICE CODE: B

CUSTOMIZE IT!

ORDER TOLL FREE 1■800■533■4350   24-HOUR FAX ORDERING   1■800■344■4293

PLAN NP1349

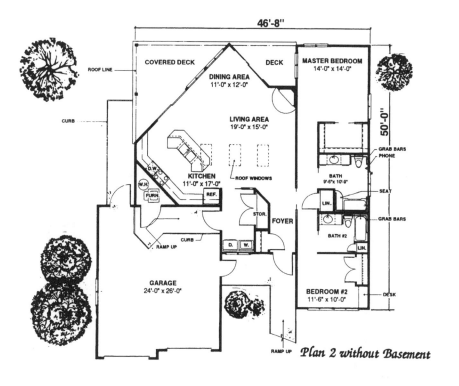

46'-8"

COVERED DECK
ROOF LINE
DECK
MASTER BEDROOM
14'-0" x 14'-0"

DINING AREA
11'-0" x 12'-0"

CURB

LIVING AREA
19'-0" x 15'-0"

50'-0"

GRAB BARS
PHONE

BATH
9'-6"x 10'-9"

SEAT

KITCHEN
11'-0" x 17'-0"

ROOF WINDOWS

D.W.
W.H.
FURN.
REF.

LIN.
STOR.
FOYER

GRAB BARS

BATH #2

RAMP UP
CURB

D.   W.

LIN.

GARAGE
24'-0" x 26'-0"

BEDROOM #2
11'-6" x 10'-0"

DESK

RAMP UP

Plan 2 without Basement

Paramount Estate

Features

- Striking contemporary design offers complete handicap accessibility.
- Deep, two-car garage offers ramp access into utility room.
- Main entryway is via ramped front porch into foyer.
- Foyer leads to a combined kitchen/ dining/living area illuminated by three large roof windows.
- Rear of home features two, separate covered decks for ultimate in relaxation and outdoor leisure.
- Both bathrooms, located in right wing, feature grab bars and sliding door access.

Total Living Area   1,340 sq. ft.

PRICE CODE: B

64

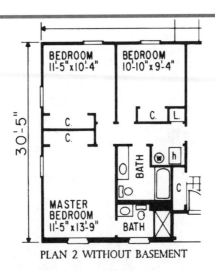

PLAN 2 WITHOUT BASEMENT

BEDROOM
11'-5" x 10'-4"

BEDROOM
10'-10" x 9'-4"

30'-5"

C.

C.

C.

L.

BATH

W

h

MASTER
BEDROOM
11'-5" x 13'-9"

BATH

C

Country Ranch

Features

• Brick front combined with wooden siding adds elegant touch to this colonial ranch.

• Front porch adds a touch of easy, country living to this home.

• Enter from the porch directly to the impressive great room with fireplace with open floor plan to dining room.

• Left wing includes master bedroom with private bath, and two additional bedrooms with full bath.

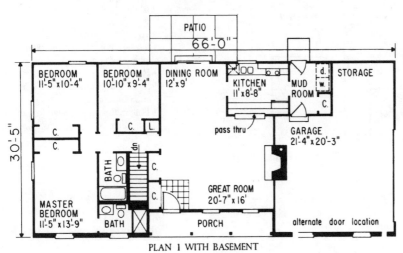

PATIO

66'-0"

BEDROOM
11'-5" x 10'-4"

BEDROOM
10'-10" x 9'-4"

DINING ROOM
12' x 9'

KITCHEN
11' x 8'-8"

MUD
ROOM

d.

w.

STORAGE

C.

30'-5"

C.

C.

C.

L.

pass thru

BATH

C.

GARAGE
21'-4" x 20'-3"

MASTER
BEDROOM
11'-5" x 13'-9"

C.

BATH

GREAT ROOM
20'-7" x 16'

PORCH

alternate door location

PLAN 1 WITH BASEMENT

Total Living Area   1,345 sq. ft.

PRICE CODE: B

PLAN FD6953

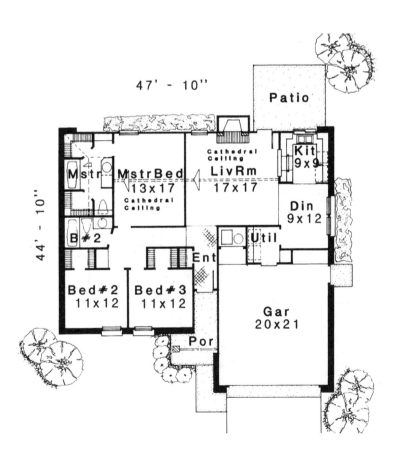

47' - 10''

44' - 10''

Patio

Mstr

MstrBed
13x17
Cathedral
Ceiling

B#2

Cathedral
Ceiling

LivRm
17x17

Kit
9x9

Din
9x12

Util

Ent

Bed #2
11x12

Bed #3
11x12

Gar
20x21

Por

Total Living Area   1,345 sq. ft.

PRICE CODE: B

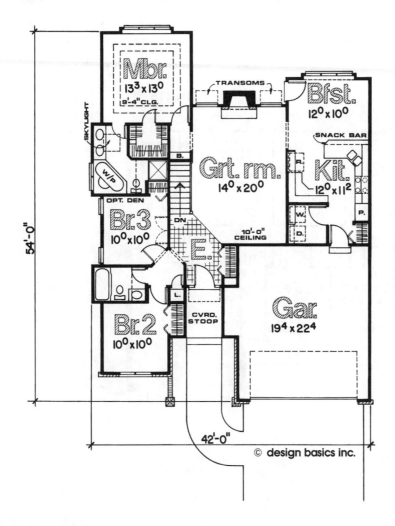

Mbr.
13³ x 13⁰
9'-4" CLG.

TRANSOMS

Bfst.
12⁰ x 10⁰

SKYLIGHT

SNACK BAR

Grt. rm.
14⁰ x 20⁰

Kit.
12⁰ x 11²

OPT. DEN

Br. 3
10⁰ x 10⁰

DN

10'-0"
CEILING

Br. 2
10⁰ x 10⁰

CVRD.
STOOP

Gar.
19⁴ x 22⁴

54'-0"

42'-0"

© design basics inc.

Features

- Open staircase for versatile future finished basement.
- Picture windows with transoms above flank handsome fireplace in great room.
- Snack bar and pantry in open kitchen.
- Closet at utility entrance through garage.
- Bright windows for views out the back of dinette.
- Bedroom #3 easily becomes den.
- Boxed window, built-in bookcase and tiered ceiling for master bedroom.
- Skylit dressing/bath area features double vanity and whirlpool on angle under window.

Total Living Area   1,347 sq. ft.

PRICE CODE: C

CUSTOMIZE IT!

ORDER TOLL FREE   1▪800▪533▪4350   24-HOUR FAX ORDERING   1▪800▪344▪4293

PLAN MN1353

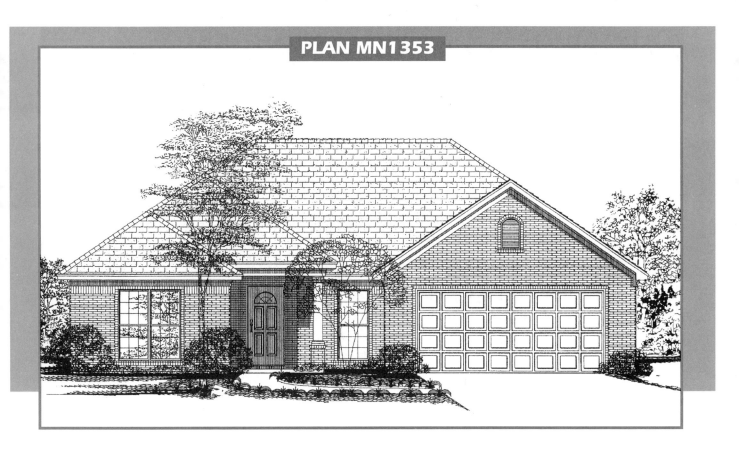

48-2

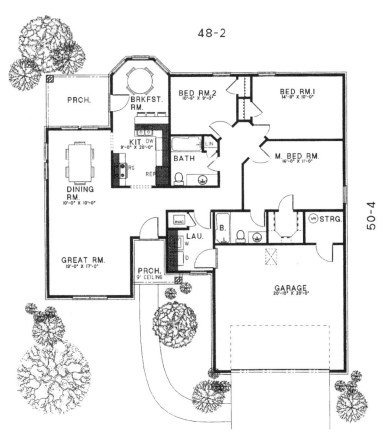

50-4

67

PRCH.

BRKFST. RM.

BED RM.2
10'-6" X 9'-0"

BED RM.1
14'-8" X 10'-0"

KIT.
9'-0" X 20'-0"
DW

RG
REF.

BATH
LIN

M. BED RM.
16'-0" X 11'-0"

DINING RM.
10'-0" X 10'-0"

HVAC

LAU.
W
D

B.

STRG.

GREAT RM.
13'-0" X 17'-0"

PRCH.
9' CEILING

GARAGE
20'-10" X 20'-0"

Total Living Area   **1,353 sq. ft.**

PRICE CODE: B

C U S T O M I Z E   I T !

ORDER TOLL FREE   1 ▪ 800 ▪ 533 ▪ 4350   **24-HOUR FAX ORDERING**   1 ▪ 800 ▪ 344 ▪ 4293

PLAN NP WOODRIDGE

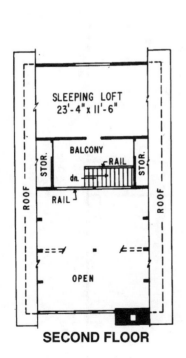

SECOND FLOOR

SLEEPING LOFT
23'-4" x 11'-6"

STOR.
BALCONY
RAIL
dn.
STOR.
ROOF
ROOF
RAIL

OPEN

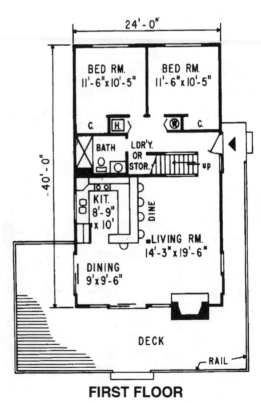

FIRST FLOOR

24'-0"

BED RM.
11'-6"x10'-5"

BED RM.
11'-6"x10'-5"

C.   H.   W.   C.

BATH
LDR'Y.
OR
STOR.
up

KIT.
8'-9"
x 10'

DINE

LIVING RM.
14'-3"x19'-6"

DINING
9'x9'-6"

40'-0"

DECK

RAIL

First Floor	960 sq. ft.
Second Floor	394 sq. ft.
Total Living Area	1,354 sq. ft.

PRICE CODE: B

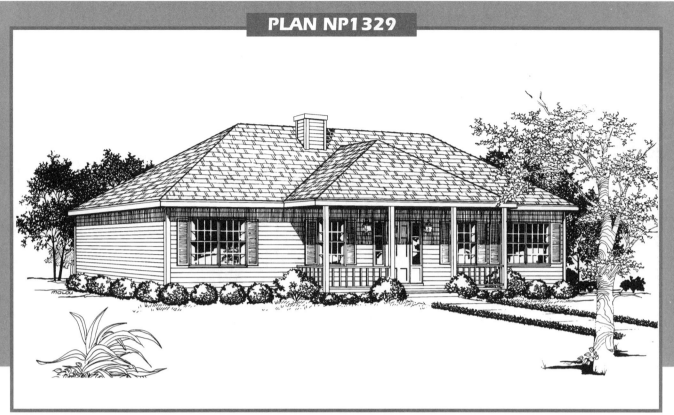

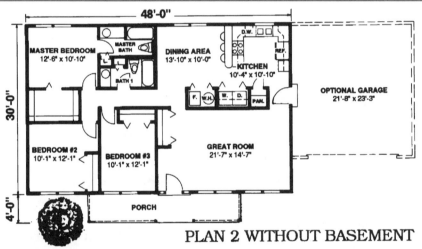

PLAN 2 WITHOUT BASEMENT

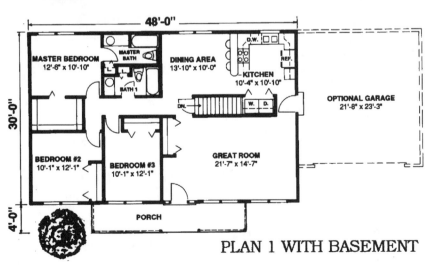

PLAN 1 WITH BASEMENT

Country Sprite

Features

- This home is an excellent choice for the first-time home buyer.
- Optional garage and optional front porch allow you to expand as your budget allows.
- U-shaped kitchen and dining area at rear of home.
- Master bedroom with private bath.
- Two additional bedrooms share one full bath.

Total Living Area   1,364 sq. ft.

PRICE CODE: B

69

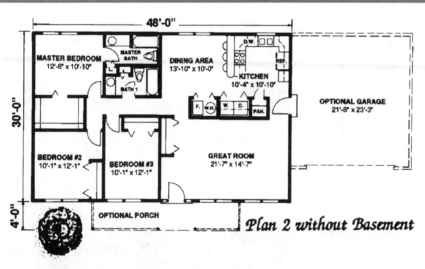

Plan 2 without Basement

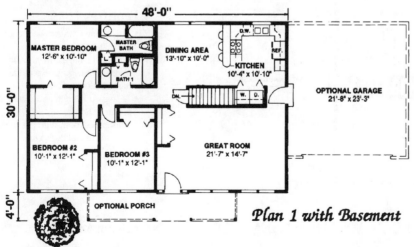

Plan 1 with Basement

Country Bower

Features

- Excellent choice for first-time home buyer.
- Optional garage and optional front porch let you add to your home as your budget allows.
- Enter through the large great room in the right wing.
- U- shaped kitchen with dining area located at the rear.
- Two bedrooms share a full bath.
- Master bedroom with large walk-in closet and full bath.

Total Living Area   1,364 sq. ft.

PRICE CODE: B

CUSTOMIZE IT!

ORDER TOLL FREE   1▪800▪533▪4350   24-HOUR FAX ORDERING   1▪800▪344▪4293

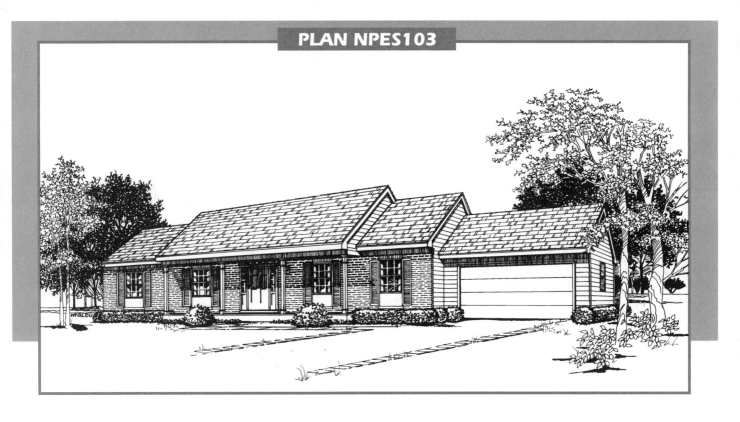

71

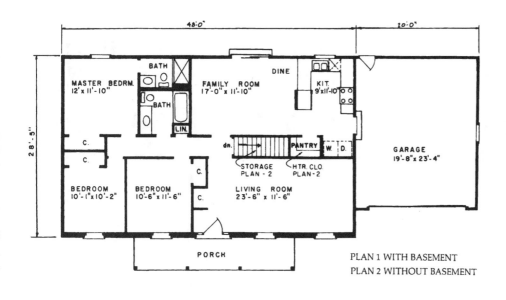

MASTER BEDRM.
12' x 11'-10"

BATH

FAMILY ROOM
17'-0" x 11'-10"

DINE

KIT.
9'x11'-10"

BATH

LIN.

C.

C.

dn.

STORAGE
PLAN - 2

PANTRY

HTR. CLO.
PLAN - 2

W. D.

GARAGE
19'-8" x 23'-4"

BEDROOM
10'-1" x 10'-2"

BEDROOM
10'-6" x 11'-6"

C.

C.

LIVING ROOM
23'-6" x 11'-6"

PORCH

48'-0"

10'-0"

28'-5"

PLAN 1 WITH BASEMENT
PLAN 2 WITHOUT BASEMENT

Features

- The look of an estate home with an affordable price tag! The U-shaped kitchen has an adjacent dining area and family room.
- Three bedrooms are clustered in the left wing.
- The master bedroom features a private bath while the other two bedrooms share a full bath.
- Truss roof construction allows you to adjust for varying roof loads

Total Living Area   1,364 sq. ft.

PRICE CODE: B

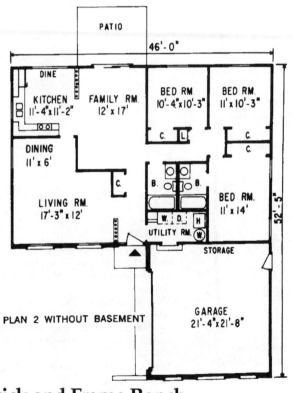

PLAN 2 WITHOUT BASEMENT

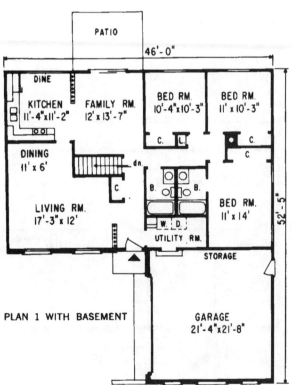

PLAN 1 WITH BASEMENT

Brick and Frame Ranch

Features

- Cozy, efficient comfort is the key in this home.
- Three bedrooms with two full baths.
- Living/dining room combination.
- Efficiently sized kitchen.
- Family room opens to backyard patio.

Total Living Area   1,380 sq. ft.

PRICE CODE: B

PLAN NP GREELEY

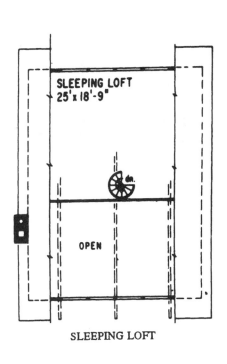

SLEEPING LOFT
25' x 18'-9"

OPEN

SLEEPING LOFT

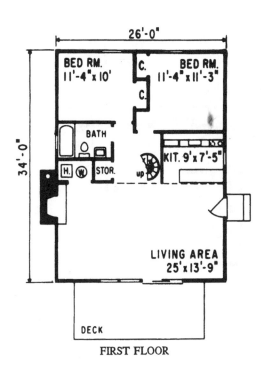

26'-0"

BED RM.
11'-4" x 10'

C.

BED RM.
11'-4" x 11'-3"

C.

34'-0"

BATH

KIT. 9' x 7'-5"

H. W. STOR.

up

LIVING AREA
25' x 13'-9"

DECK

FIRST FLOOR

First Floor	884 sq. ft.
Second Floor	507 sq. ft.
Total Living Area	1,391 sq. ft.

PRICE CODE: B

CUSTOMIZE IT!

ORDER TOLL FREE 1 ▪ 800 ▪ 533 ▪ 4350   24-HOUR FAX ORDERING 1 ▪ 800 ▪ 344 ▪ 4293

74

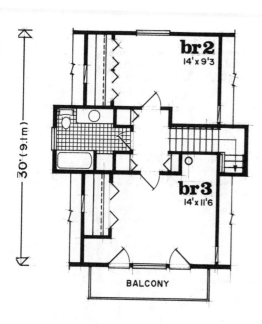

SECOND LEVEL 584 sq.ft. (54.3 m²)

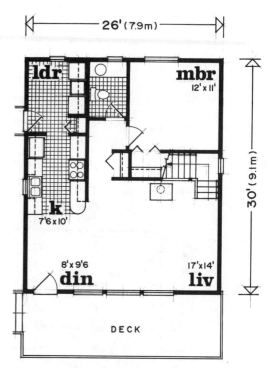

FIRST LEVEL 780 sq.ft. (72.5 m²)

Features

- A-frame cottage takes full advantage of a front view.
- Side entrance has direct access to the laundry/mud room.
- Galley style kitchen, offers an abundance of counter and cupboard space.

- Open dining and living rooms stretch out to the front deck, extending living space.
- Main floor master bedroom enjoys privacy.
- Bedroom 2 boasts a double wall closet while bedroom 3 has a private balcony.

Total Living Area **1,410 sq. ft.**

PRICE CODE: B

CUSTOMIZE IT!

ORDER TOLL FREE 1 ■ 800 ■ 533 ■ 4350   **24-HOUR FAX ORDERING** 1 ■ 800 ■ 344 ■ 4293

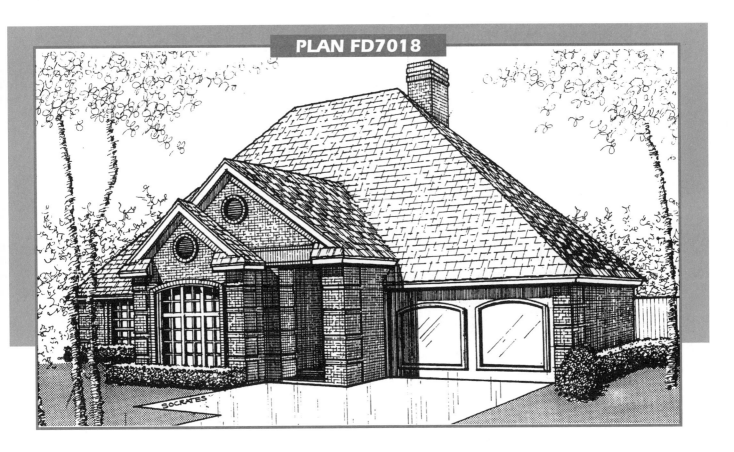

PLAN FD7018

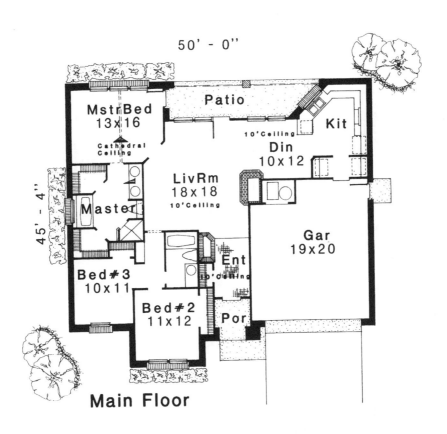

50' - 0"

75

45' - 4"

MstrBed 13 x 16
Cathedral Ceiling

Patio

Kit

10'Ceiling

Din 10 x 12

Master

LivRm 18 x 18
10'Ceiling

Gar 19 x 20

Bed #3 10 x 11

Ent
10'Ceiling

Bed #2 11 x 12

Por

Main Floor

Total Living Area   1,417 sq. ft.

PRICE CODE: B

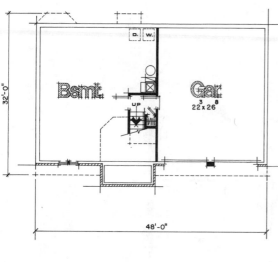

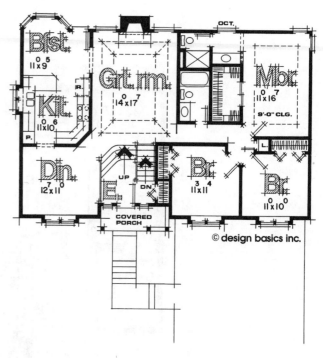

© design basics inc.

76

Features

- Optional elevation included with this plan at no additional cost.
- Formal dining room opens to large entry with coat closet and wide stairs.
- Great room with vaulted ceiling and fireplace as focal point.
- Double L-shaped kitchen includes boxed window at sink, pantry, space saver microwave and buffet counter.
- Convenient split-entry ranch design.
- Core hallway opens to large master bedroom with walk-in closet and private bath.
- Secondary bedrooms feature boxed windows and share centrally located hall bath.

Total Living Area   **1,429 sq. ft.**

PRICE CODE: C

CUSTOMIZE IT!

ORDER TOLL FREE   **1■800■533■4350**   24-HOUR FAX ORDERING   **1■800■344■4293**

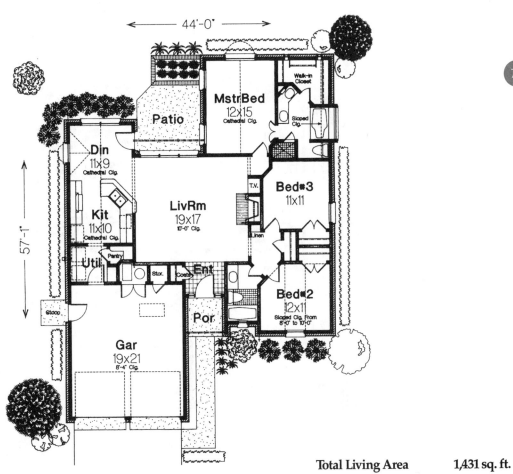

Total Living Area   1,431 sq. ft.

PRICE CODE: B

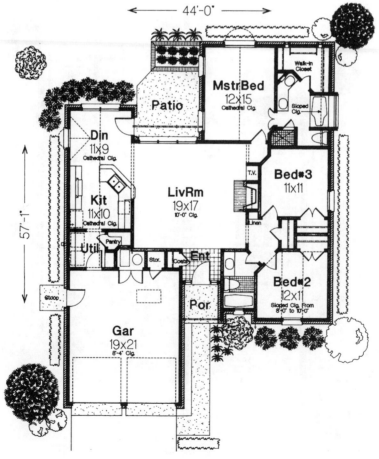

44'-0"

57'-1"

Patio

MstrBed
12x15
Cathedral Clg.

Walk-in Closet

Sloped Clg.

Din
11x9
Cathedral Clg.

LivRm
19x17
10'-0" Clg.

T.V.

Bed#3
11x11

Kit
11x10
Cathedral Clg.

Linen

Pantry

Util

Stor.

Closet

Ent

Bed#2
12x11
Sloped Clg. From 8'-0" to 10'-0"

Stoop

Por.

Gar
19x21
8'-4" Clg.

Total Living Area   1,431 sq. ft.

PRICE CODE: B

Plan 2 without Basement

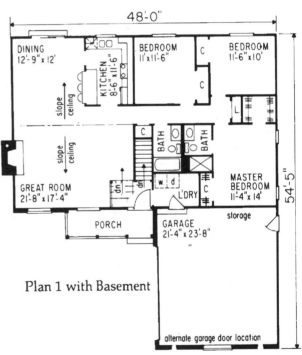

Plan 1 with Basement

Harrow Wood Lodge

Features

- Colonial ranch design offers many amenities.
- Small porch gives a cozy welcome feeling to front entrance.
- Sunken great room with sloped ceiling features fireplace.
- Back-to-back full baths serve the three bedrooms.

- Kitchen with breakfast island adjoins dining room.

Total Living Area   1,440 sq. ft.

PRICE CODE: B

CUSTOMIZE IT!

ORDER TOLL FREE   1 ▪ 800 ▪ 533 ▪ 4350   24-HOUR FAX ORDERING   1 ▪ 800 ▪ 344 ▪ 4293

80

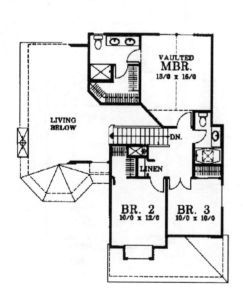

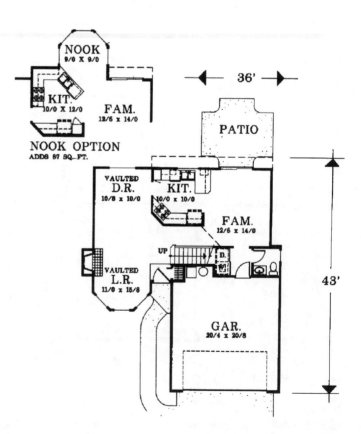

Total Living Area   1,468 sq. ft.

81

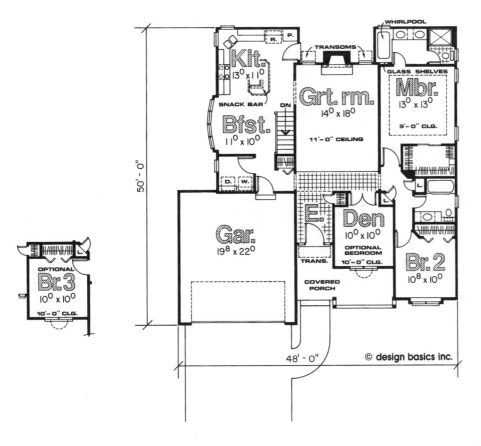

Features

- Covered porch adds charm to this ranch home.
- Sunny great room with 11-foot ceiling open to entry.
- Bowed breakfast area open to kitchen including island snack bar, corner sink and access to back yard.
- Secondary bedrooms share hall bath.
- Den with 10-foot-high ceiling and French doors options as a third bedroom.
- Volume master suite features whirlpool bath, dual lavs and mirrored doors to walk-in closet.

Total Living Area   1,479 sq. ft.

PRICE CODE: C

82

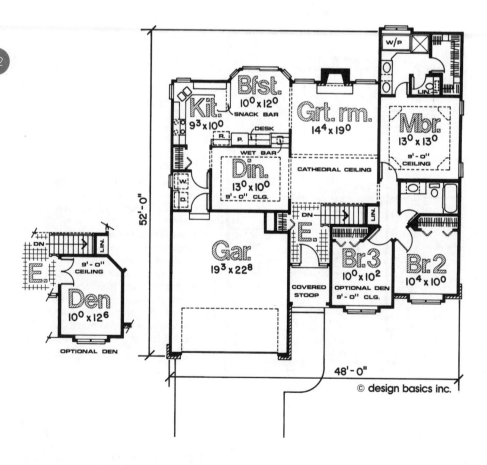

OPTIONAL DEN

© design basics inc.

Features

- Sleek lines of this ideally compact ranch allude to sophistication within.
- Tiled entry views spacious great room with window-framed fireplace.
- Dining area strategic to great room enhances formal or family gatherings.
- Kitchen/breakfast area designed for enjoyment has utility room nearby.
- Bedroom #3 designed for optional conversion to a den or home office.
- Comfortable secondary bedrooms share nearby bath and hall linen closet.
- Luxurious master suite enjoys sunlit whirlpool, dual lav dressing area and roomy walk-in closet .

Total Living Area   1,496 sq. ft.

PRICE CODE: C

83

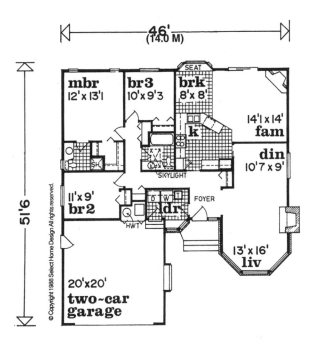

46'
(14.0 M)

51'6

mbr 12' x 13'1

br3 10'x 9'3

brk 8'x 8'

SEAT

k

14'1 x 14' **fam**

din 10'7 x 9'

SKYLIGHT

FOYER

br 2 11'x 9'

ldr

HWT

13' x 16' **liv**

20'x20' **two~car garage**

1496 sq. ft.

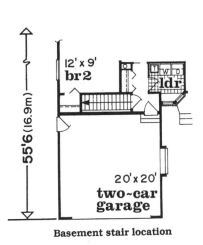

55'6 (16.9m)

br 2 12' x 9'

ldr

20' x 20' **two~car garage**

Basement stair location

Features

- Living room rests in a windowed-bay.
- Open plan kitchen has ample counter space.
- Cozy window seat tucked in the breakfast bay.
- Fireplace warms the family room.
- Master bedroom has a walk-in wardrobe and three-piece ensuite with shower.
- Main bathroom has a skylight.
- Plan includes a basement and crawlspace foundation.

Total Living Area	1,496 sq. ft.

PRICE CODE: B

PLAN 2 WITHOUT BASEMENT

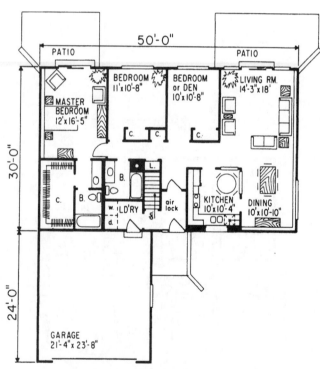

PLAN 1 WITH BASEMENT

Shady Berm

Features

- Attractive berm at front of home adds appeal to this visually distinctive home.
- Open floor plan provides for fast and efficient air and heat circulation.
- South facing living room and bedrooms get the most of light and warmth from winter sun.

- Kitchen includes dining area with adjacent dining room.
- Living room open from dining room with rear access to patio.
- Large master bedroom includes walk-in closet and vanity with private tub and toilet.

Total Living Area   **1,500 sq. ft.**

PRICE CODE: B

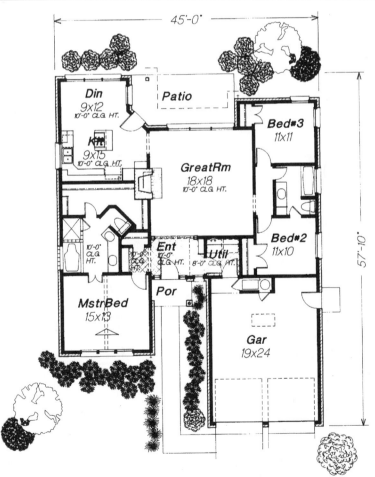

Total Living Area   1,505 sq. ft.

PRICE CODE: B

PLAN NP1185

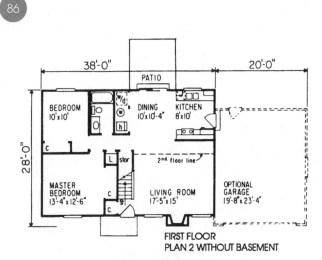

FIRST FLOOR
PLAN 2 WITHOUT BASEMENT

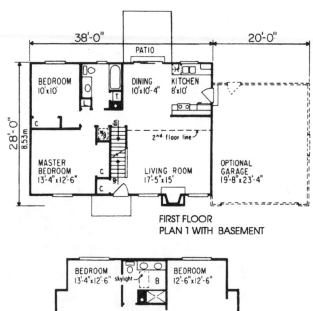

FIRST FLOOR
PLAN 1 WITH BASEMENT

SECOND FLOOR

Quantico

Features

- Compact and stylish, this home is perfect for those with a limited budget.
- The two-car garage is optional and can be added later.
- Front door opens to a spacious living room with cathedral ceiling.

- Efficient kitchen with access outside or to optional garage.
- Second floor includes two bedrooms with full bath and skylight.

First Floor	988 sq. ft.
Second Floor	520 sq. ft.
Total Living Area	1,508 sq. ft.

PRICE CODE: B

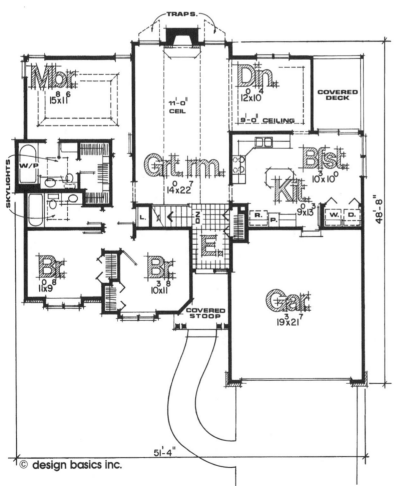

Features

- Dramatic high entry framed by columns and windows.
- Expansive great room features sloped ceilings to 11 feet and impressive fireplace surrounded by windows.
- Complete island kitchen includes lazy Susan, pantry and desk plus adjacent laundry area.
- Bright breakfast eating area.
- Formal ceiling in dining room.
- Vaulted ceiling in master bedroom with corner windows.
- Master bath features skylight and walk-in closet.
- Pleasant window sills in front bedrooms.

Total Living Area   1,511 sq. ft.

PRICE CODE: C

PLAN NP TIDEWATER

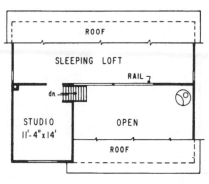

**SECOND FLOOR
STUDIO AND LOFT**

CROSS SECTION

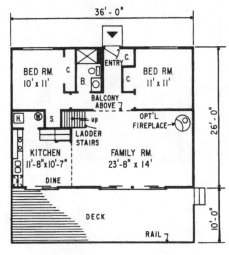

FIRST FLOOR

First Floor	936 sq. ft.
Second Floor	592 sq. ft.
Total Living Area	1,528 sq. ft.

PRICE CODE: B

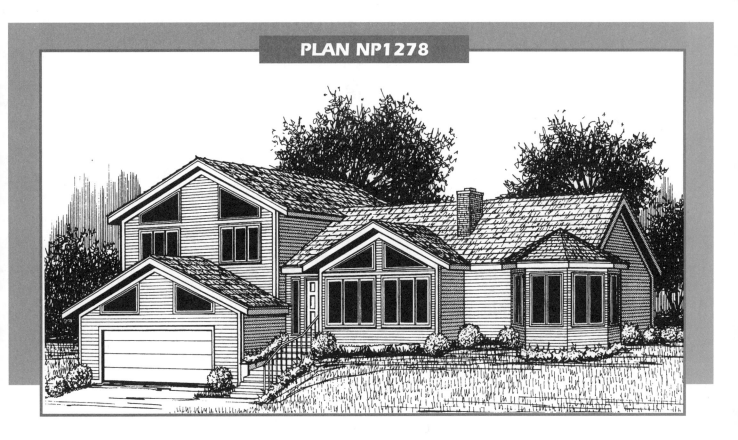

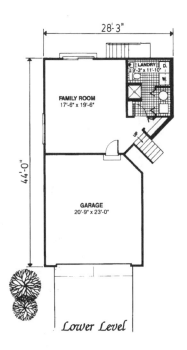

28'-3"

LANDRY.
9'-3" x 11'-10"

FAMILY ROOM
17'-6" x 19'-6"

44'-0"

GARAGE
20'-9" x 23'-0"

Lower Level

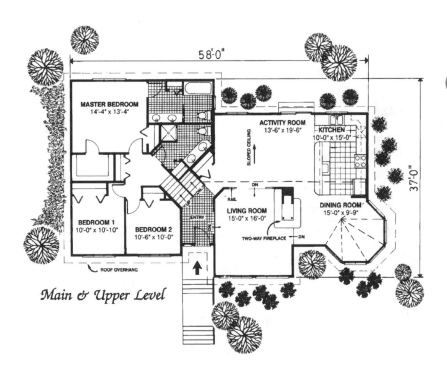

58'-0"

MASTER BEDROOM
14'-4" x 13'-4"

ACTIVITY ROOM
13'-6" x 19'-6"

KITCHEN
10'-0" x 15'-0"

SLOPED CEILING

37'-0"

DN

BEDROOM 1
10'-0" x 10'-10"

BEDROOM 2
10'-6" x 10'-0"

ENTRY

LIVING ROOM
15'-0" x 16'-0"

RAIL

DINING ROOM
15'-0" x 9'-9"

TWO-WAY FIREPLACE

DN

ROOF OVERHANG

Main & Upper Level

Casa Rustique

Features

- This rustic, split-level home includes many outstanding features, such as wide roof overhangs and vertical windows.
- Master bedroom with compartmented bath and large walk-in closet.
- Two additional bedrooms share a deluxe bath.

- Sunken living room features two-way fireplace and entry to dining room with beautiful, huge circular windows.
- Sloped, cathedral-ceiling in the activity room.
- Entry down to lower level, where the large family room and laundry room is located.

Main Level	1,645 sq. ft.
Lower Level	520 sq. ft.
Total Living Area	2,165 sq. ft.

PRICE CODE: B

45'6
(13.9 M)

90

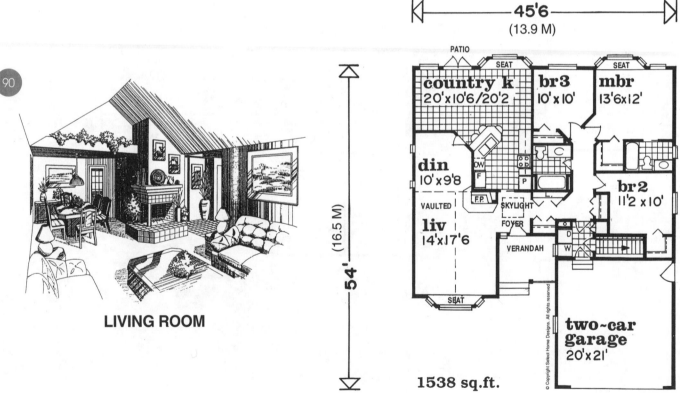

LIVING ROOM

54' (16.5 M)

PATIO

SEAT · SEAT

country k
20'x10'6/20'2

br3
10' x 10'

mbr
13'6x12'

din
10' x 9'8

DW

F

P

br2
11'2 x 10'

VAULTED

liv
14'x17'6

F.P.

SKYLIGHT

FOYER

D

W

SEAT

VERANDAH

two~car garage
20'x21'

1538 sq.ft.

Features

- Compact three bedroom or two bedroom plus den design offers all the amenities.
- Skylit foyer spills to a vaulted living room with bay window seat; open end fireplace warms this area.
- Country kitchen has a breakfast bar, window seat, double door access to the patio and abundant space for a large table.

- Master bedroom has a walk-in closet, window seat and three piece bathroom with soaking tub.

Total Living Area: 1,538 sq. ft.

PRICE CODE: B

CUSTOMIZE IT!

ORDER TOLL FREE 1·800·533·4350 **24-HOUR FAX ORDERING** 1·800·344·4293

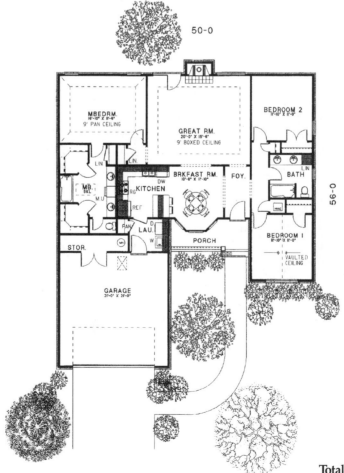

50-0

56-0

MBEDRM.
18'-10" X 11'-6"
9' PAN CEILING

GREAT RM.
20'-0" X 15'-6"
9' BOXED CEILING

BEDROOM 2
11'-10" X 11'-0"

MB.
9'-0"

M.U.

LIN.

LIN.

KITCHEN

BRKFAST RM.
10'-6" X 11'-10"

FOY.

BATH

LIN.

REF.

DW

RG

HVAC

FAN

D

LAU.

W

PORCH

BEDROOM 1
11'-10" X 11'-0"

STOR.

VAULTED
CEILING

GARAGE
21'-0" X 21'-0"

91

Total Living Area   1,538 sq. ft.

PRICE CODE: B

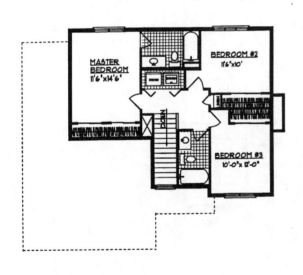

SECOND FLOOR PLAN

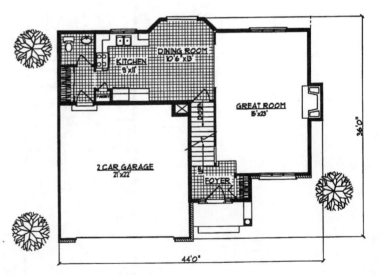

MAIN FLOOR PLAN

First Floor	811 sq. ft.
Second Floor	741 sq. ft.
Total Living Area	1,552 sq. ft.

PRICE CODE: B

PLAN FD7406

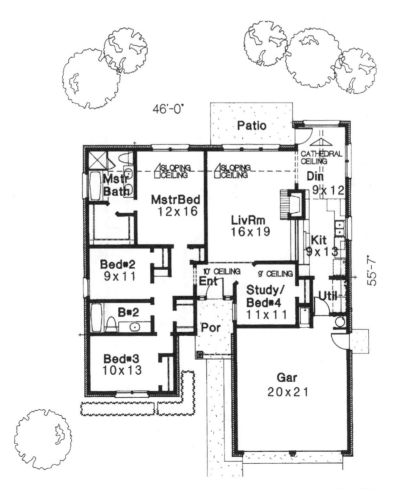

46'-0"

Patio

CATHEDRAL CEILING

Mstr Bath

SLOPING CEILING | SLOPING CEILING

MstrBed 12x16

Din 9x12

LivRm 16x19

Kit 9x13

Bed#2 9x11

10' CEILING | 9' CEILING

Ent

Study/ Bed#4 11x11

Util

B#2

Por

Bed#3 10x13

Gar 20x21

55'-7"

Total Living Area   1,561 sq. ft.

PRICE CODE: B

94

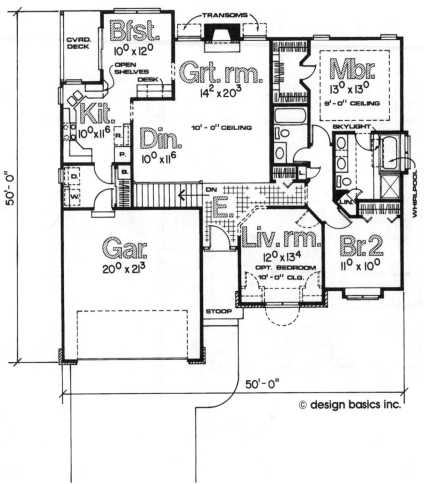

OPEN SHELVES

DESK

© design basics inc.

Features

- Volume entry with transoms above door offers view of great room fireplace.
- Formal living room converts to optional third bedroom.
- Kitchen features pantry, lazy Susan and corner sink with windows.
- Breakfast area has built-in desk and access to covered deck or great room.
- Laundry room with closet serves as mud entry from garage.
- Master bedroom features clever indented walk-in closet.
- Master bath includes whirlpool tub separated from shower by glass panel, double vanity and skylight.

Total Living Area   1,561 sq. ft.

PRICE CODE: C

Covered Patio

Sitting Area
8'-0" Clg.

Bed#2
15x11
8'-0" Clg.

Walk-In Closet

Walk-In Closet

Kit
11x12
10'-0" Clg.

Brkfst
10x11
10'-0" Clg.

MstrBed
14x19
9'-0" Vaulted Clg.

10'-0" Clg.

Linen

Bed#3
11x10
8'-0" Clg.

Util

Ent
10'-0" Clg.

Coats

Sloped Clg.

Walk-In Closet

LivRm
16x19
Cathedral Clg.

Books

Books

Por

Gar
19x24

50'-0"

57'-10"

© Copyright Fillmore Designs Group

Total Living Area   1,573 sq. ft.

PRICE CODE: B

C U S T O M I Z E   I T !

ORDER TOLL FREE   1▪800▪533▪4350   24-HOUR FAX ORDERING   1▪800▪344▪4293

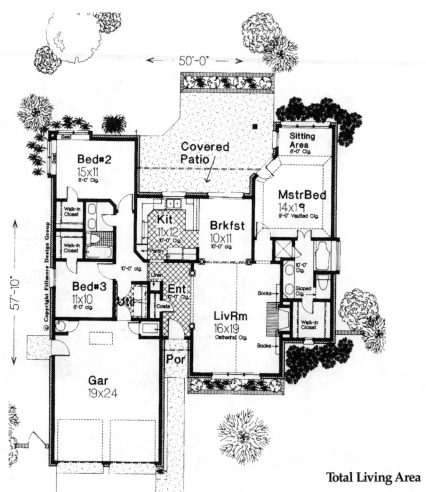

50'-0"

57'-10"

© Copyright Fillmore Design Group

Covered Patio

Sitting Area
8'-0" Clg.

Bed#2
15x11
8'-0" Clg.

Walk-In Closet

Walk-In Closet

MstrBed
14x19
9'-0" Vaulted Clg.

Kit
11x12
10'-0" Clg.

Brkfst
10x11
10'-0" Clg.

Pantry

Linen

10'-0" Clg.

10'-0" Clg.

Sloped Clg.

Books

Walk-In Closet

Bed#3
11x10
8'-0" Clg.

Util

Ent
10'-0" Clg.

Coats

LivRm
16x19
Cathedral Clg.

Books

Por

Gar
19x24

Total Living Area 1,573 sq. ft.

PRICE CODE: B

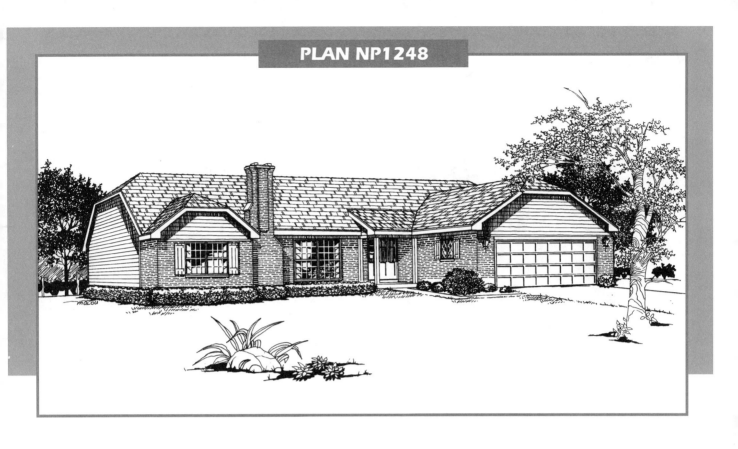

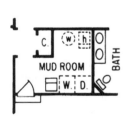

PLAN 2 WITHOUT BASEMENT

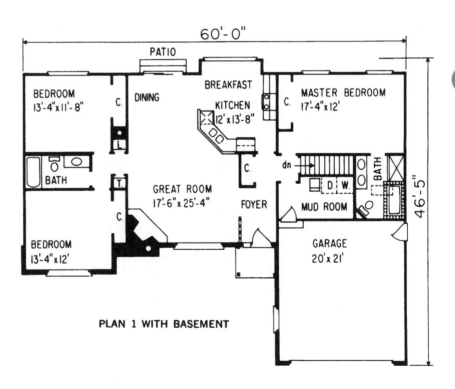

PLAN 1 WITH BASEMENT

Morning Glory

Features

- Distinctive one-story home with efficient floor plan.
- Foyer enters into open great room with corner fireplace and rear dining room with adjoining kitchen.
- Left wing includes two bedrooms with full bath.
- Right wing includes master bedroom with full bath.
- Garage access to home enters mud room/laundry.

Total Living Area   1,574 sq. ft.

PRICE CODE: B

CUSTOMIZE IT!

ORDER TOLL FREE   1■800■533■4350   24-HOUR FAX ORDERING   1■800■344■4293

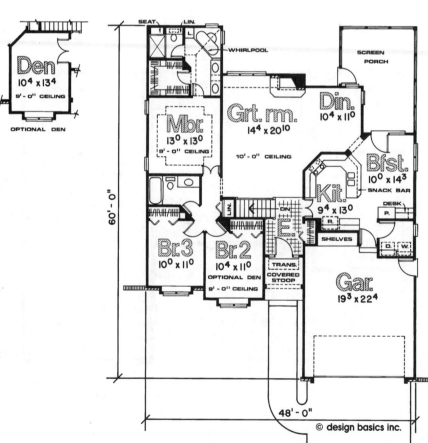

Den
10⁴ x 13⁴
9' - 0" CEILING

OPTIONAL DEN

SEAT LIN.

WHIRLPOOL

SCREEN
PORCH

Mbr.
13⁰ x 13⁰
9' - 0" CEILING

Grt. rm.
14⁴ x 20¹⁰
10' - 0" CEILING

Din.
10⁴ x 11⁰

Bfst.
10⁰ x 14³

Kit.
9⁴ x 13⁰

SNACK BAR

DESK

P.

R.

SHELVES

D. W

LIN.

DN

Br.3
10⁰ x 11⁰

Br.2
10⁴ x 11⁰
OPTIONAL DEN
9' - 0" CEILING

TRANS.
COVERED
STOOP

Gar.
19³ x 22⁴

60' - 0"

48' - 0"

© design basics inc.

Features
- Brick wing walls provide visually expansive front elevation.
- From entry, traffic flows into bright great room with impressive 2-sided fireplace.
- Dining room opens to great room, offering view of fireplace.
- French doors off entry open into kitchen.
- Kitchen features large pantry, planning desk and snack bar.
- Dinette accesses large, comfortable screen porch.
- Laundry room is strategically located off kitchen and provides for direct access from garage.
- Built-in shelves in garage.
- French doors access master suite with formal ceiling and pampering bath.

Total Living Area   **1,580 sq. ft.**

CUSTOMIZE IT!

ORDER TOLL FREE   1 ▪ 800 ▪ 533 ▪ 4350   24-HOUR FAX ORDERING   1 ▪ 800 ▪ 344 ▪ 4293

PLAN DB2324

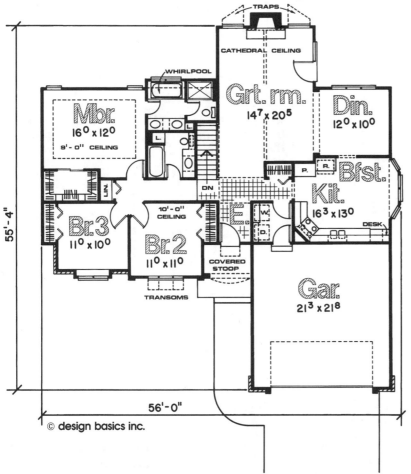

TRAPS

WHIRLPOOL

CATHEDRAL CEILING

Mbr.
16⁰ x 12⁰
9'-0" CEILING

Grt. rm.
14⁷ x 20⁵

Din.
12⁰ x 10⁰

Bfst.

Kit.
16³ x 13⁰

DESK

DN

10'-0" CEILING

Br.3
11⁰ x 10⁰

Br.2
11⁰ x 11⁰

COVERED STOOP

TRANSOMS

Gar.
21³ x 21⁸

55'-4"

56'-0"

© design basics inc.

Features

- Crisp lines with subtle detailing enhance front elevation of this elegant ranch.
- Striking 10-foot-high entry has plant shelf integrated above closet.
- Cathedral ceiling and fireplace flanked by trapezoid windows highlight great room.
- Expansive great room, dining room, sunny kitchen/breakfast area encourage leisure and entertaining pursuits.
- Luxurious master suite benefits from ceiling detail and spacious walk-in closet with mirrored doors.
- Compartmented master bath features window to flood whirlpool and vanity/makeup area with natural light.

Total Living Area   **1,583 sq. ft.**

PRICE CODE: C

CUSTOMIZE IT!

ORDER TOLL FREE   1▪800▪533▪4350   24-HOUR FAX ORDERING   1▪800▪344▪4293

PLAN DB2526

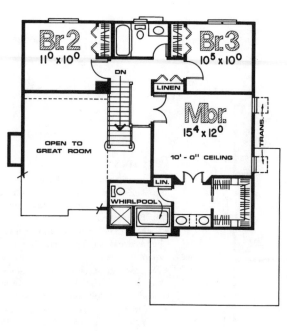

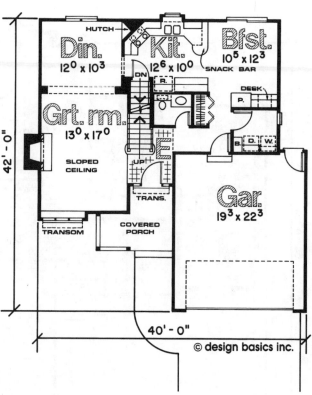

Features

- Gabled roof, brick accents and covered front porch combine to present striking elevation.
- Ceiling slopes from 9 foot to 16'-10", plus raised hearth fireplace of great room makes dramatic presentation.
- Formal dining room features built-in hutch.
- Efficient kitchen with snack bar serves dinette, which has planning desk and large pantry.

- Laundry area has window, broom closet and hanging rod.
- French doors access master suite with 10-foot-high ceiling, and second set of French doors lead to private dressing area with dual lavs.
- Natural light floods master bath above whirlpool tub.

First Floor	845 sq. ft.
Second Floor	760 sq. ft.
Total Living Area	1,605 sq. ft.

PRICE CODE: C

CUSTOMIZE IT!

ORDER TOLL FREE 1■800■533■4350   24-HOUR FAX ORDERING 1■800■344■4293

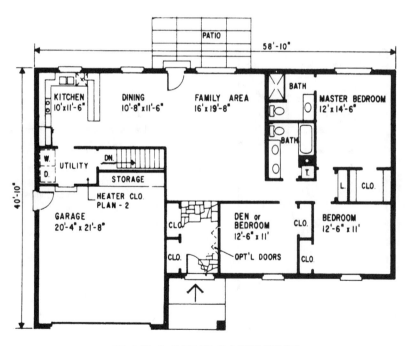

PLAN 1 WITH BASEMENT
PLAN 2 WITHOUT BASEMENT

Features

- This 1605 square foot energy-savings design offers plenty of storage space and is an ideal starter home.
- Three bedrooms are clustered in the right wing with the master bedroom served by its own bath and walk-in closet.
- Entry foyer has two closets for your convenience and opens into large family area.
- Two car garage contains storage and work area.
- Truss roof construction allows you to adjust for varying roof loads.

| Plan 1 or 2 | 1,605 sq. ft. |
| Plan 3 or 4 | 1,620 sq. ft. |

PRICE CODE: B

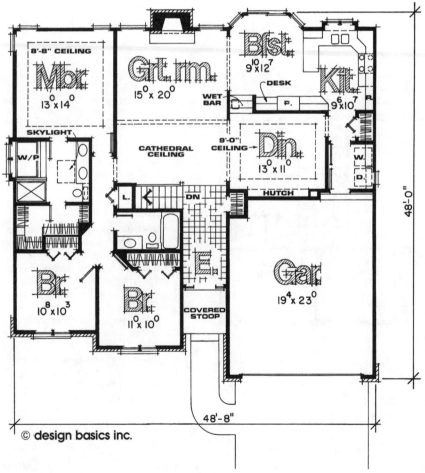

© design basics inc.

Features

- Large volume great room with fireplace flanked by windows to the back seen from entry.
- See-thru wet bar between dinette and dining room with formal ceiling.
- Fully-equipped kitchen with desk, pantry and special window box above sink.
- Secondary bedrooms share convenient hall bath.
- Roomy master suite with volume ceiling equipped with special amenities including skylit dressing/bath area with plant shelf, large walk-in closet, double vanity and whirlpool tub.
- Extra deep garage.

Total Living Area   **1,604 sq. ft.**

PRICE CODE: C

PLAN FD7099

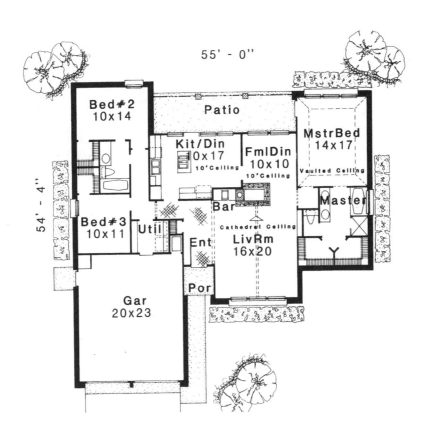

55' - 0''

54' - 4''

Bed #2
10x14

Patio

Kit/Din
10x17
10'Ceiling

FmlDin
10x10
10'Ceiling

MstrBed
14x17
Vaulted Ceiling

Bed #3
10x11

Util

Bar

Master

Ent

LivRm
16x20
Cathedral Ceiling

Por

Gar
20x23

Total Living Area   1,624 sq. ft.

PRICE CODE: B

104

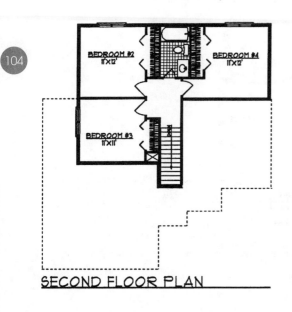

SECOND FLOOR PLAN

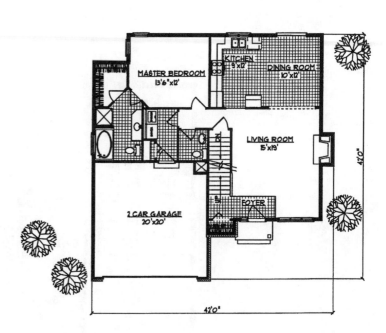

MAIN FLOOR PLAN

First Floor	1,011 sq. ft.
Second Floor	621 sq. ft.
Total Living Area	1,632 sq. ft.

PRICE CODE: B

PLAN AM2126B

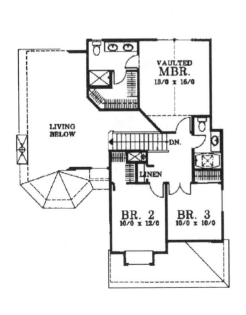

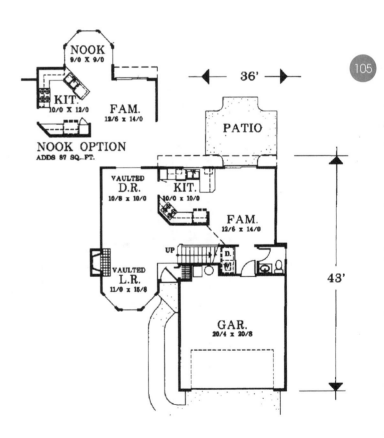

NOOK
9/0 X 9/0

KIT.
10/0 X 12/0

FAM.
12/6 x 14/0

NOOK OPTION
ADDS 87 SQ. FT.

VAULTED
MBR.
13/6 x 15/0

LIVING
BELOW

DN.

LINEN

BR. 2
10/0 x 12/0

BR. 3
10/0 x 10/0

36'

PATIO

VAULTED
D.R.
10/8 x 10/0

KIT.
10/0 x 10/0

FAM.
12/6 x 14/0

UP

D.

VAULTED
L.R.
11/0 x 15/8

GAR.
20/4 x 20/8

43'

105

Total Living Area 1,636 sq. ft.

PRICE CODE: B

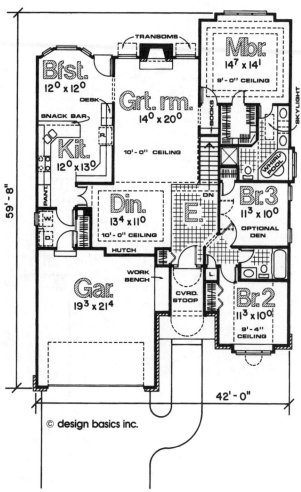

© design basics inc.

59'- 8"

42'- 0"

Bfst. 12⁰ x 12⁰

Grt. rm. 14⁰ x 20⁰
10'- 0" CEILING

Mbr. 14⁷ x 14¹
9'- 0" CEILING

TRANSOMS

DESK

SNACK BAR

Kit. 12⁰ x 13⁰

SKYLIGHT

BOOKS

WHIRL POOL

Din. 13⁴ x 11⁰
10'- 0" CEILING

E.

Br.3 11³ x 10⁰

OPTIONAL DEN

HUTCH

PANT.

W.
D.

Gar. 19³ x 21⁴

WORK BENCH

CVRD. STOOP

Br.2 11³ x 10⁰
9'- 4" CEILING

Features

- Barrel vaulted porch highlights elevation of this comfortable ranch.
- Great room features cozy fireplace flanked by bright windows.
- Gourmet kitchen and bayed dinette includes snack bar for additional eating space, wrapping counters, planning desk and access to outdoors.
- Secondary bedrooms share bath; bedroom #3 designed as optional den.
- Master bedroom features tiered ceiling, bright window design and an ample walk-in closet.
- Master dressing/bath area includes skylight, his and her vanities and corner whirlpool.

Total Living Area   **1,636 sq. ft.**

PRICE CODE: C

CUSTOMIZE IT!

ORDER TOLL FREE   1 ▪ 800 ▪ 533 ▪ 4350   24-HOUR FAX ORDERING   1 ▪ 800 ▪ 344 ▪ 4293

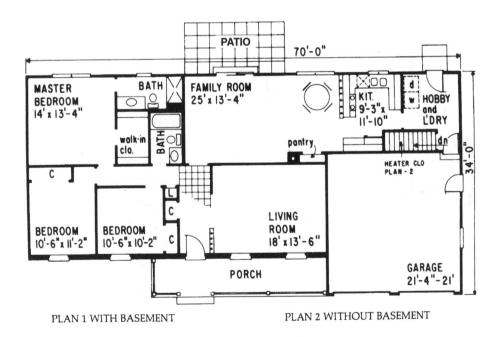

PLAN 1 WITH BASEMENT   PLAN 2 WITHOUT BASEMENT

Accent Ranch

Features

- Attractive front entry porch with railing adds to country appeal in this home.
- Long family room is located at front of house.
- Family room with dining area adjacent to kitchen situated at rear of home.
- Hobby room/laundry separate kitchen and garage.
- Left wing includes master bedroom with private bath and two additional bedrooms with full bath.

Total Living Area   1,643 sq. ft.

PRICE CODE: B

PLAN SH1189-1650

© Copyright Select Home Designs. All rights reserved.

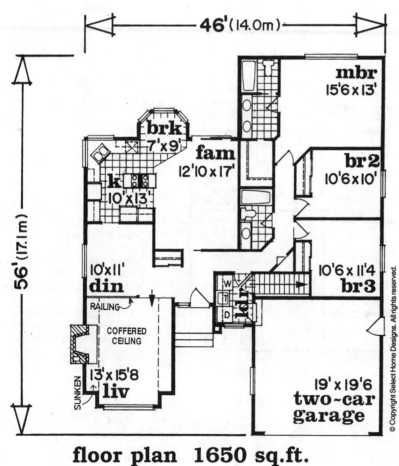

46' (14.0m)

56' (17.1m)

mbr
15'6 x 13'

brk
7' x 9'

fam
12'10 x 17'

br2
10'6 x 10'

k
10' x 13'

br3
10'6 x 11'4

10'x11'
din

RAILING

COFFERED CEILING

W
D

13' x 15'8
liv

SUNKEN

19' x 19'6
two~car garage

© Copyright Select Home Designs. All rights reserved.

floor plan 1650 sq.ft.

Features

- Design may be finished in either brick, siding or stucco.
- Roof line and windows differ with each elevation.
- Sunken living room, with masonry fireplace, is separated from dining room by low railing.
- Kitchen, with centre cooking island, serves breakfast bay.
- Large family room has sliding glass walk-through to patio.
- Master bedroom features walk-in closet and three-piece ensuite, with twin vanity and separate toilet and shower.

Total Living Area   1,650 sq. ft.

PRICE CODE: B

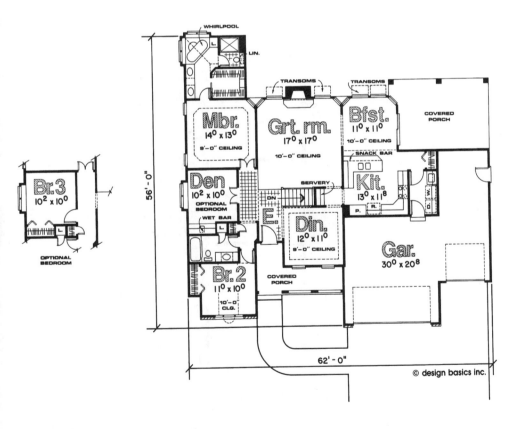

109

Features

- Covered front porch with wood railing combines with covered rear porch to expand living space outside.
- Handy servery located between volume dining room and expansive great room with high windows flanking fireplace.
- Laundry room with sink and hanging rods doubles as mud entrance from outside.
- Well-planned kitchen has generous pantry and snack bar.
- Den with wet bar enhances privacy of master suite or can be converted to optional third bedroom.
- Accessed via French doors, volume master suite includes walk-in closet, compartmented stool and shower, and corner whirlpool.

Total Living Area   **1,651 sq. ft.**

PRICE CODE: C

PLAN NP1295

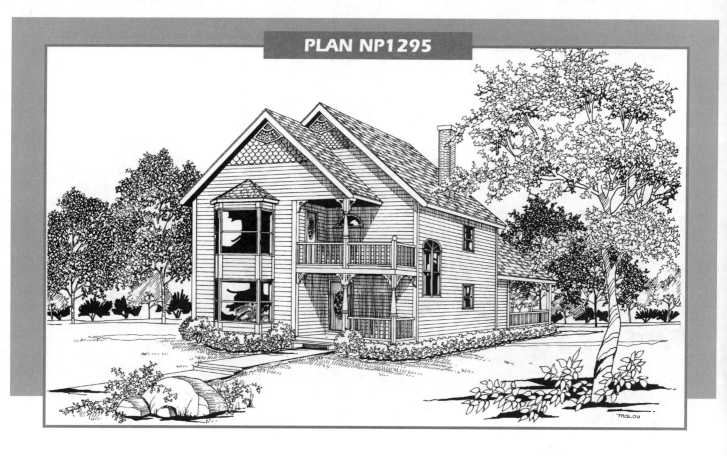

110

BEDROOM 2
10'-8" x 10'-0"

BENCH

BATH

DN.

MASTER BEDROOM
13'-0" x 14'-7"

BALCONY

Second Floor

26'-0"

DN.

FAMILY ROOM
13'-0" x 11'-6"

P.R.

BACK PORCH

44'-0"

DINING ROOM
13'-0" x 10'-0"

REF.

KITCHEN
8'-3" x 10'-0"

PANTRY

ACTIVITY AREA
13'-0" x 17'-1"

DN.

UP

VERANDA

DN.

First Floor

First Floor	1,092 sq. ft.
Second Floor	570 sq. ft.
Total Living Area	1,662 sq. ft.

PRICE CODE: B

111

Total Living Area   1,662 sq. ft.

PRICE CODE: B

Total Living Area   1,662 sq. ft.

PRICE CODE: B

CUSTOMIZE IT!

ORDER TOLL FREE   1▪800▪533▪4350   24-HOUR FAX ORDERING   1▪800▪344▪4293

113

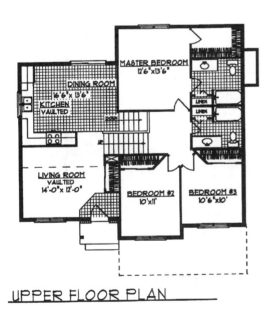

UPPER FLOOR PLAN

- MASTER BEDROOM 12'6"x13'6"
- DINING ROOM 16'6"x13'6"
- KITCHEN VAULTED
- LINEN
- LINEN
- LIVING ROOM VAULTED 14'-0"x12'-0"
- BEDROOM #2 10'x11'
- BEDROOM #3 10'6"x10'

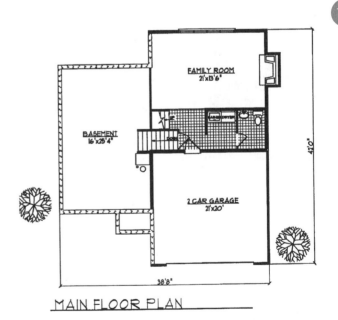

MAIN FLOOR PLAN

- FAMILY ROOM 21'x13'6"
- BASEMENT 16'x25'4"
- 2 CAR GARAGE 21'x20'
- 41'0"
- 38'8"

First Floor	449 sq. ft.
Second Floor	1,214 sq. ft.
Total Living Area	1,663 sq. ft.

PRICE CODE: B

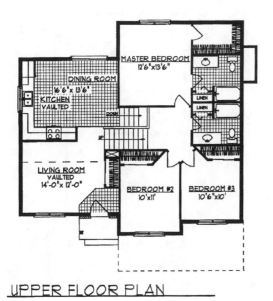

UPPER FLOOR PLAN

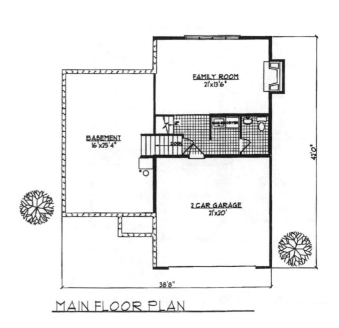

MAIN FLOOR PLAN

First Floor	449 sq. ft.
Second Floor	1,214 sq. ft.
Total Living Area	1,663 sq. ft.

PRICE CODE: B

PLAN AM2126C

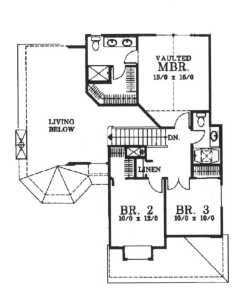

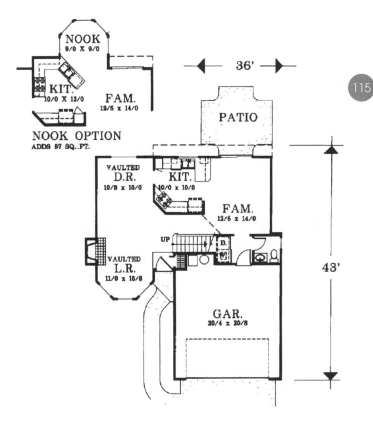

NOOK OPTION
ADDS 57 SQ. FT.

115

THE OPTIONS SHOWN ABOVE ALL INCORPORATE
THE NOOK BAY AND OTHER MINOR CHANGES
REQUIRED TO CHANGE THE ELEVATION.

First Floor	748 sq. ft.
Second Floor	720 sq. ft.
Total Living Area	1,663 sq. ft.

PRICE CODE: B

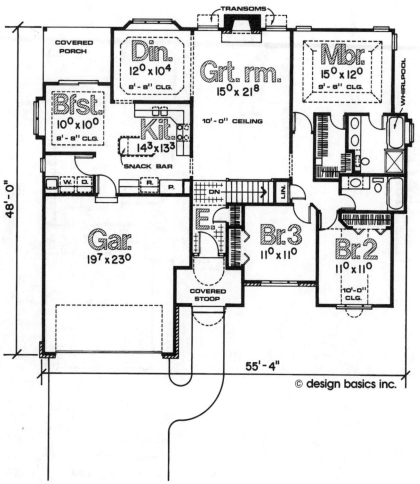

© design basics inc.

Features

- Brick and stucco enhance the dramatic front elevation showcased by sleek lines and decorative windows.
- Inviting entry with view into great room is enhanced by arched window and plant shelves above.
- Fireplace in great room framed by sunny windows with transoms above.
- Bayed window dining room nestled between great room and superb kitchen/breakfast area.
- Design of sleeping areas places buffer between secondary bedrooms and master suite.
- Peaceful master suite enjoys vaulted ceiling, roomy walk-in closet and sunlit master bath with dual lavs and whirlpool.

Total Living Area   1,666 sq. ft.

PRICE CODE: C

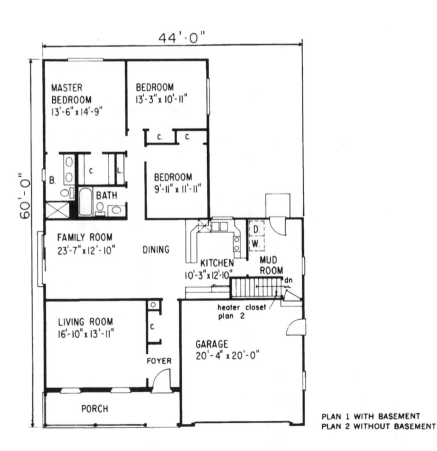

44'-0"

60'-0"

MASTER
BEDROOM
13'-6" x 14'-9"

BEDROOM
13'-3" x 10'-11"

c.   c.

BATH
B.   c.   L.

BEDROOM
9'-11" x 11'-11"

FAMILY ROOM
23'-7" x 12'-10"

DINING

D.
W.

MUD
ROOM

KITCHEN
10'-3" x 12'-10"

dn

heater closet
plan 2

LIVING ROOM
16'-10" x 13'-11"

c.

GARAGE
20'-4" x 20'-0"

FOYER

PORCH

PLAN 1 WITH BASEMENT
PLAN 2 WITHOUT BASEMENT

Simply Country

Features

- Simple but attractive styling in this ranch home perfect for a narrow lot.
- Front entry porch with entrance foyer with closet opens to living room.
- Garage entrance to home leads to kitchen through mud room/laundry.
- U-shaped kitchen opens to dining area and family room.
- Three bedrooms are situated at the rear of the home with two full baths.
- Master bedroom has walk-in closet.

Total Living Area   1,668 sq. ft.

PRICE CODE: B

CUSTOMIZE IT!

ORDER TOLL FREE   1■800■533■4350   24-HOUR FAX ORDERING   1■800■344■4293

118

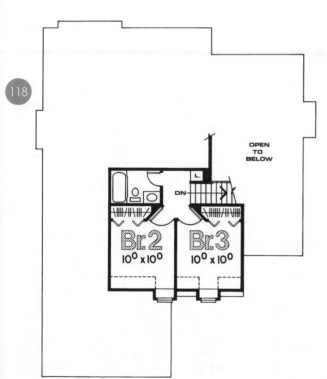

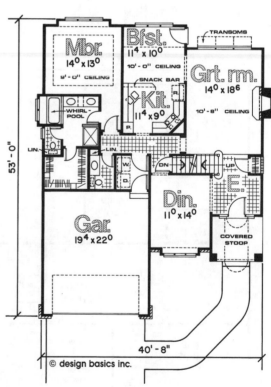

© design basics inc.

Features

- Suited for narrow lots, this home demonstrates design efficiency.
- Off entry, wide-cased opening leads to bright formal dining room.
- Volume entry is accented by glass blocks that spotlight decorator plant shelf above guest coat closet.
- Great room with its 10'-8" ceiling, full wall of windows and brick fireplace create inviting atmosphere.
- Dinette achieves light, open sensation with its 10-foot ceiling and large windows.
- Master bedroom, with its 9-foot boxed ceiling and expansive window area, affords maximum privacy.

First Floor	**1,327 sq. ft.**
Second Floor	**348 sq. ft.**
Total Living Area	**1,675 sq. ft.**

PRICE CODE: C

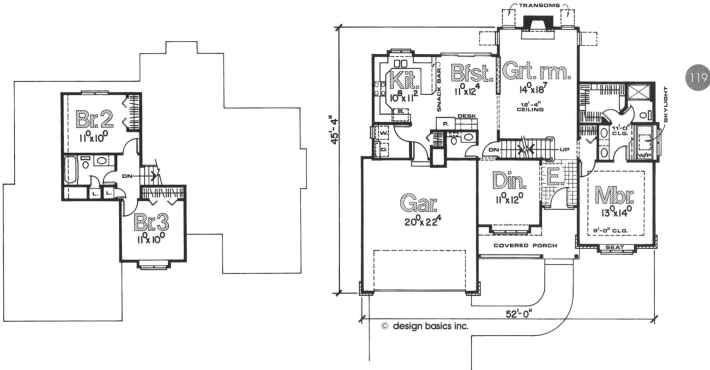

© design basics inc.

Features

- Welcoming covered porch.
- Entry views formal dining room with boxed window and great room beyond.
- Beautiful fireplace flanked by tall corner windows in volume great room.
- Powder bath conveniently located.
- Closet at garage entry.
- Window in laundry room.

- Open kitchen/dinette area features pantry, desk and snack bar counter.
- Elegant master suite with formal ceiling detail and window seat.
- Skylight above whirlpool, decorator plant shelf and double lavs in deluxe master dressing area.
- Secondary bedrooms share centrally located bathroom.

First Floor	**1,297 sq. ft.**
Second Floor	**388 sq. ft.**
Total Living Area	**1,685 sq. ft.**

PRICE CODE: C

CUSTOMIZE IT!

ORDER TOLL FREE 1 ▪ 800 ▪ 533 ▪ 4350   24-HOUR FAX ORDERING   1 ▪ 800 ▪ 344 ▪ 4293

PLAN AM2126D

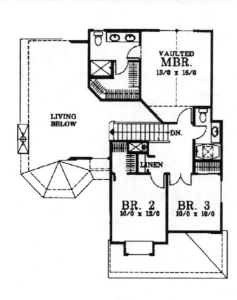

VAULTED MBR.
13/6 x 16/0

LIVING BELOW

DN.

LINEN

BR. 2
10/0 x 12/0

BR. 3
10/0 x 10/0

NOOK
9/0 X 9/0

KIT.
10/0 X 12/0

FAM.
12/6 x 14/0

NOOK OPTION
ADDS 87 SQ. FT.

◄— 36' —►

PATIO

VAULTED D.R.
10/6 x 10/0

KIT.
10/0 x 10/0

FAM.
12/6 x 14/0

UP

VAULTED L.R.
11/0 x 15/6

GAR.
20/4 x 20/8

43'

THE OPTIONS SHOWN ABOVE ALL INCORPORATE
THE NOOK BAY AND OTHER MINOR CHANGES
REQUIRED TO CHANGE THE ELEVATION.

First Floor	**748 sq. ft.**
Second Floor	**720 sq. ft.**
Total Living Area	**1,686 sq. ft.**

PRICE CODE: B

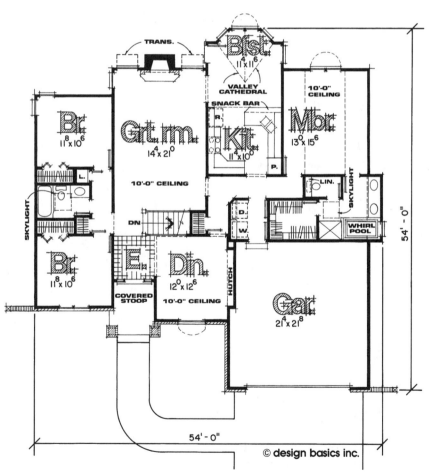

© design basics inc.

54' - 0"

Features

- Volume dining room with hutch space and elegant arched window open to entry.
- Expansive great room with 10-foot ceiling offers brick fireplace framed by windows to the back.
- Bayed window in breakfast area which features sloped ceiling.
- Garage accesses home through conveniently located laundry room .
- Master bedroom with volume ceiling brightened by arched transom window.
- Skylit dressing/bath area includes double vanity, walk-in closet, whirlpool tub and plant ledge.
- Secondary bedrooms share skylit bath.

Total Living Area   **1,697 sq. ft.**

PRICE CODE: C

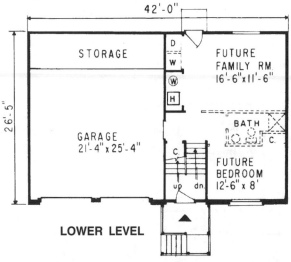

LOWER LEVEL

42'-0"

26'-5"

STORAGE

GARAGE
21'-4" x 25'-4"

D
W
W
H

FUTURE
FAMILY RM.
16'-6"x11'-6"

BATH

FUTURE
BEDROOM
12'-6" x 8'

up   dn.

122

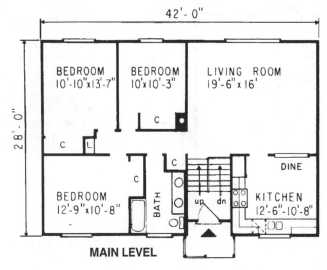

MAIN LEVEL

42'-0"

28'-0"

BEDROOM
10'-10"x13'-7"

BEDROOM
10'x10'-3"

LIVING ROOM
19'-6"x16'

BEDROOM
12'-9"x10'-8"

BATH

DINE

KITCHEN
12'-6"-10'-8"

up   dn

Features
- This contemporary bi-level allows for future expansion as your family grows.
- Energy-saving designs feature three bedrooms clustered at left wing of main level.
- One full bath serves all bedrooms.
- Two-car garage is located on lower level.
- Truss roof construction allows adjustment for different roof loads.

Main level	1,164 sq. ft.
Lower Level	534 sq. ft.
Total Living Area	1,698 sq. ft.

PRICE CODE: B

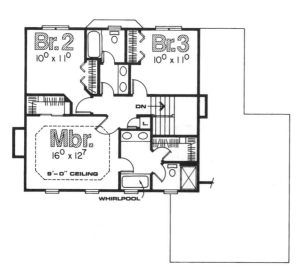

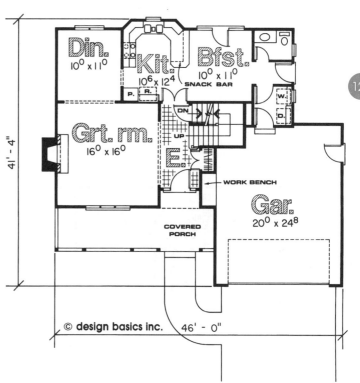

123

© design basics inc.

Features

- Traditional elevation with covered porch provides mass appeal.
- U-stairs and French doors highlight entry.
- Large cased openings define formal dining room and great room without restricting space.
- Bayed kitchen and breakfast area have functional access to utility area and side yard.
- Secondary bedrooms share generous compartmented bath with dual lavs.
- His and her walk-in closets, 9-foot-high boxed ceiling and whirlpool bath create stately master suite.
- Workbench and extra storage space in garage.

First Floor	904 sq. ft.
Second Floor	796 sq. ft.
Total Living Area	1,700 sq. ft.

PRICE CODE: C

CUSTOMIZE IT!

ORDER TOLL FREE 1 ▪ 800 ▪ 533 ▪ 4350   24-HOUR FAX ORDERING 1 ▪ 800 ▪ 344 ▪ 4293

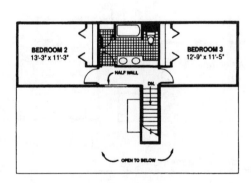

Second Floor

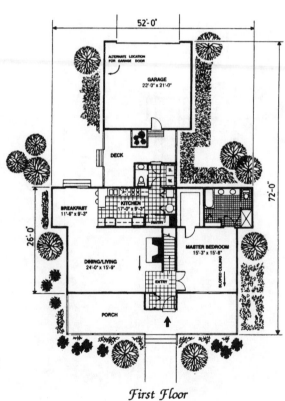

First Floor

Sunnybrooke

Features

- Traditional 1-1/2 story home with covered entrance porch sure to please the most exacting family.
- Designed to enhance an outdoor lifestyle.
- Variable roof lines with wide overhangs provide shade and protection from the elements.
- Central kitchen with breakfast nook/snack bar and built-in pantry.
- Laundry room/lavatory off kitchen for extra convenience.
- First-floor master bedroom with large walk-in closet and private bath.

First Floor	1,224 sq. ft.
Second Floor	480 sq. ft.
Total Living Area	1,704 sq. ft.

PRICE CODE: B

CUSTOMIZE IT!

ORDER TOLL FREE **1▪800▪533▪4350**   24-HOUR FAX ORDERING   **1▪800▪344▪4293**

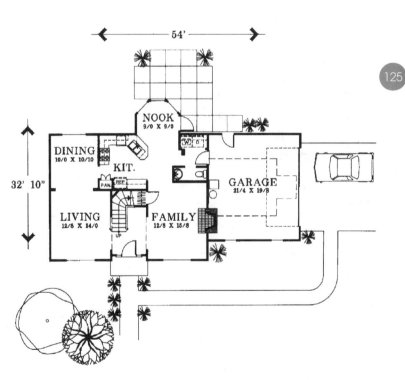

125

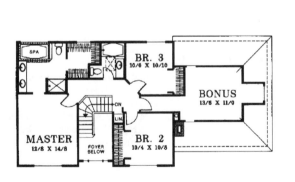

Second Floor Plan:
- SPA
- BR. 3 — 10/6 X 10/10
- BONUS — 13/6 X 11/0
- MASTER — 12/8 X 14/8
- FOYER BELOW
- BR. 2 — 10/4 X 10/8

First Floor Plan:
- 54'
- 32' 10"
- NOOK — 9/0 X 9/0
- DINING — 10/0 X 10/10
- KIT.
- PAN
- REF
- GARAGE — 21/4 X 19/8
- LIVING — 12/8 X 14/0
- FAMILY — 12/8 X 15/8
- UP

First Floor	935 sq. ft.
Second Floor	772 sq. ft.
Total Living Area	1,707 sq. ft.
Bonus Room	+177 sq. ft.

PRICE CODE: B

CUSTOMIZE IT!

ORDER TOLL FREE 1 ▪ 800 ▪ 533 ▪ 4350   **24-HOUR FAX ORDERING** 1 ▪ 800 ▪ 344 ▪ 4293

PLAN DB2355

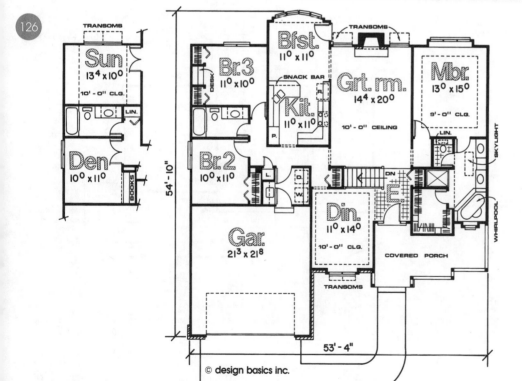

Features

- Formal dining room off entry features 10-foot walls and elegant ceiling design.
- Volume great room with raised hearth fireplace framed by sparkling windows.
- Comfortable kitchen and bowed dinette area with snack bar, pantry, lazy Susan and access for outdoor pursuits.
- Two secondary bedrooms convertible to a sun room with French doors from the dinette and an optional den.
- Bedroom #3 has built-in desk flanked by two closets.
- Secluded master suite features boxed ceiling, skylit dressing area, his and her lavs with knee space between, corner whirlpool tub and roomy walk-in closet.

Total Living Area	1,710 sq. ft.

PRICE CODE: C

PLAN FD8252-L

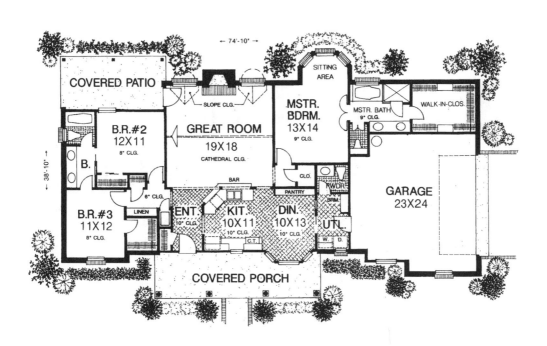

← 74'-10" →

COVERED PATIO

SITTING AREA

SLOPE CLG.

MSTR. BATH
9" CLG.

WALK-IN-CLOS.

B.R.#2
12X11
8" CLG.

GREAT ROOM
19X18
CATHEDRAL CLG.

MSTR. BDRM.
13X14
9" CLG.

38'-10"

B.

BAR

CLO.

PWDR.

GARAGE
23X24

B.R.#3
11X12
8" CLG.

LINEN

6" CLG.

ENT.
10" CLG.

KIT.
10X11
10" CLG.

PANTRY

DIN.
10X13
10" CLG.

BRM.

UTL.

C.T.

W. D.

COVERED PORCH

Total Living Area 1,724 sq. ft.

PRICE CODE: B

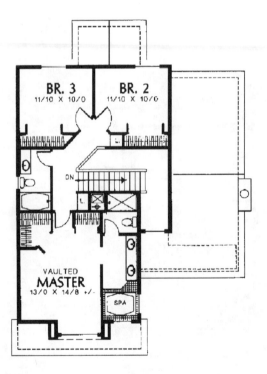

BR. 3
11/10 X 10/0

BR. 2
11/10 X 10/0

DN

VAULTED
MASTER
13/0 X 14/8 +/-

SPA

◀ 36' ▶

NOOK
9/0 X 9/0

FAMILY
14/0 X 15/8

11/0 X 12/0

VAULTED
DINING
10/6 X 10/4

50'

VAULTED
LIVING
14/8 X 14/0

W. D.

UP

GARAGE
19/4 X 21/8

PORCH

First Floor	913 sq. ft.
Second Floor	813 sq. ft.
Total Living Area	1,726 sq. ft.

PRICE CODE: B

PLAN DB2890

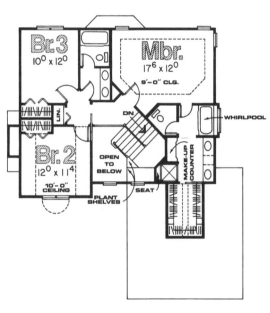

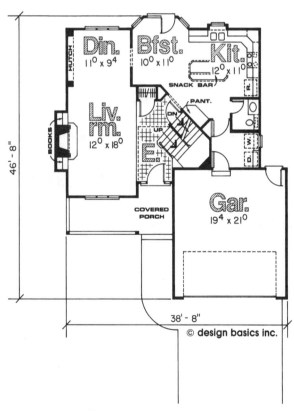

129

© design basics inc.

46' - 8"

38' - 8"

Features

- Angled U-stairs are focus for 2-story entry.
- Formal living room off entry features fireplace between built-in bookcases and view to dining room with hutch space.
- Bayed dinette adds to oversized island kitchen with large pantry, snack bar and convenient access to laundry room.
- Bedroom #2 contains beautiful arched window and volume ceiling.
- Secondary bedrooms share compartmented bath with dual lavs.
- Great master suite has whirlpool bath with dual lavs, make-up counter and generous walk-in closet.

First Floor	**884 sq. ft.**
Second Floor	**848 sq. ft.**
Total Living Area	**1,732 sq. ft.**

PRICE CODE: C

PLAN SH0-1657

130

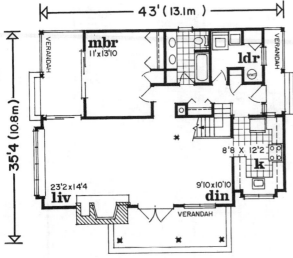

First Level 1110 square feet

- mbr 11'x13'10
- VERANDAH
- ldr
- VERANDAH
- 8'8 X 12'2
- k
- liv 23'2x14'4
- din 9'10x10'10
- VERANDAH

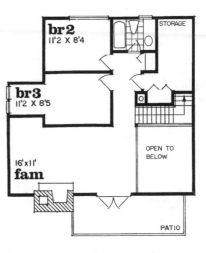

Second Level 625 square feet

- br2 11'2 X 8'4
- STORAGE
- br3 11'2 X 8'5
- OPEN TO BELOW
- fam 16'x11'
- PATIO

43' (13.1m)

35'4 (10.8m)

Features

- French doors from the covered verandah open to a spacious living room and vaulted dining room.
- Masonry fireplace, with wood storage bin, warms this area.
- Sliding glass doors from the rear verandah open to the living room and master bedroom.
- Back door has easy access to a laundry / mud room.
- Family room, with fireplace and private deck, overlooks the dining room.
- Ample storage in the second level provides an additional 105 square feet.

Dining and living room with balcony over

Total Living Area   1,735 sq. ft.

PRICE CODE: B

CUSTOMIZE IT!

ORDER TOLL FREE   1 ▪ 800 ▪ 533 ▪ 4350   24-HOUR FAX ORDERING   1 ▪ 800 ▪ 344 ▪ 4293

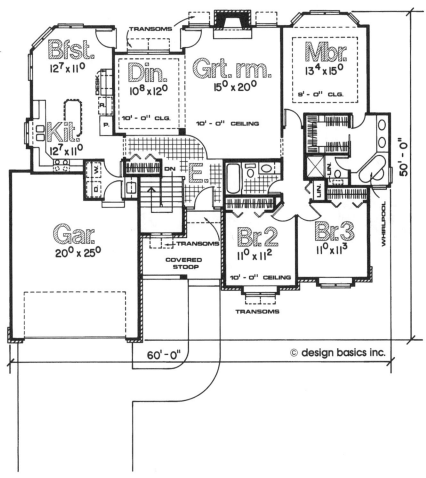

© design basics inc.

Features

- Welcoming porch at entry.
- 10-foot-high ceiling for volume in entry, great room and dining room.
- Tall windows flank the handsome fireplace seen from entry.
- Island counter, pantry, desk, and handy utility room access from kitchen.
- Open staircase with landing for possible finished basement.
- Extra length in garage for storage.
- Elegant bayed window and formal ceiling in master bedroom.
- Angled whirlpool, double vanity and walk-in closet for master dressing area.

Total Living Area   1,735 sq. ft.

PRICE CODE: C

PLAN JA5359

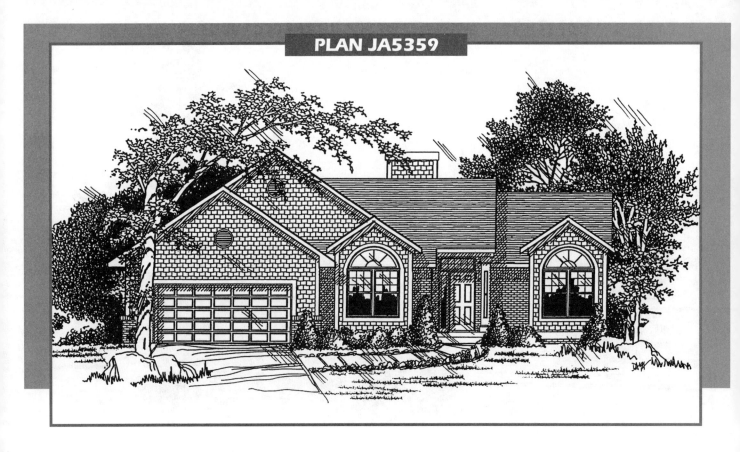

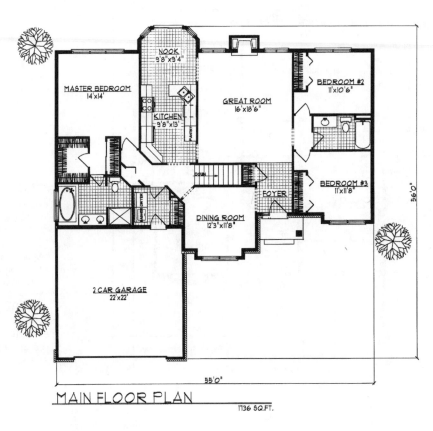

NOOK
9'8"x9'4"

MASTER BEDROOM
14'x14'

KITCHEN
9'8"x13'

GREAT ROOM
16'x18'6"

BEDROOM #2
11'x10'6"

BEDROOM #3
11'x11'8"

FOYER

DINING ROOM
12'3"x11'8"

2 CAR GARAGE
22'x22'

56'0"

55'0"

MAIN FLOOR PLAN

1736 SQ.FT.

132

Total Living Area   1,736 sq. ft.

PRICE CODE: B

PLAN FD7328

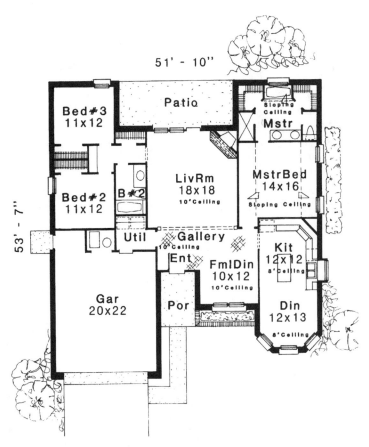

133

51' - 10''

53' - 7''

Bed #3
11x12

Patio

Sleping
Ceiling

Mstr

Bed #2
11x12

B #2

LivRm
18x18
10'Ceiling

MstrBed
14x16

Sloping Ceiling

Util

Gallery
10'Ceiling

Kit
12x12
8'Ceiling

Ent

Gar
20x22

Por

FmlDin
10x12
10'Ceiling

Din
12x13

8'Ceiling

Total Living Area   1,738 sq. ft.

CUSTOMIZE IT!

134

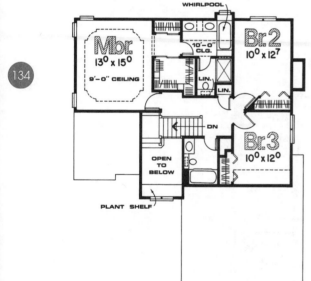

WHIRLPOOL

Mbr.
13⁰ x 15⁰

9'- 0" CEILING

Br.2
10⁰ x 12⁷

10'- 0"
CLG.

LIN.

LIN.

Br.3
10⁰ x 12⁰

OPEN
TO
BELOW

DN

PLANT SHELF

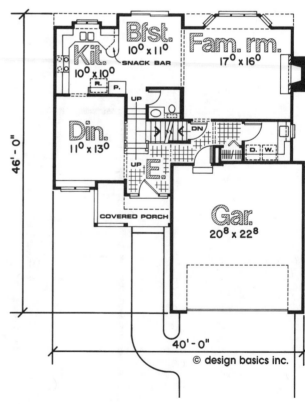

Bfst.
10⁰ x 11⁰

Kit.
10⁰ x 10⁰

SNACK BAR

Fam. rm.
17⁰ x 16⁰

R.

P.

UP

DN

46' - 0"

Din.
11⁰ x 13⁰

UP

D. W.

COVERED PORCH

Gar.
20⁸ x 22⁸

40' - 0"

© design basics inc.

Features

- Quaint front porch provides nostalgic theme to this front elevation.
- Comfort and style blend together in spacious family room with fireplace and bayed windows.
- Convenient T-shaped staircase.
- Natural light floods sizeable dining room.
- Kitchen is designed for convenience, and maximizes counter space.

- Master suite is complemented by 2 sets of mirrored by-pass doors accessing spacious closets.
- Compartmented master bath features dual lavs, whirlpool and shower with glass block accents.
- Angled openings of secondary bedrooms create interest.

First Floor	912 sq. ft.
Second Floor	827 sq. ft.
Total Living Area	1,739 sq. ft.

PRICE CODE: C

CUSTOMIZE IT!

ORDER TOLL FREE 1■800■533■4350   24-HOUR FAX ORDERING 1■800■344■4293

PLAN DB3097

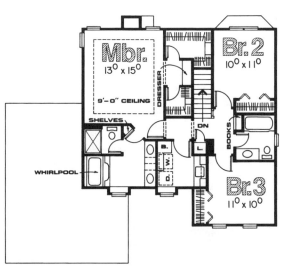

Mbr.
13⁰ x 15⁰

9'-0" CEILING

DRESSER

SHELVES

WHIRLPOOL

Br. 2
10⁰ x 11⁰

DN

BOOKS

L

D. W.

B.

Br. 3
11⁰ x 10⁰

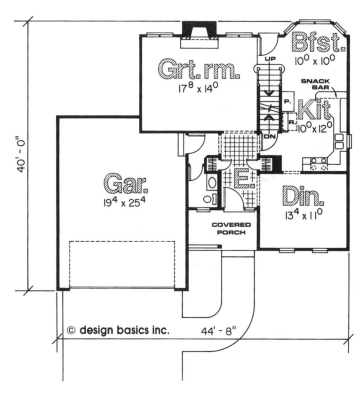

Grt. rm.
17⁸ x 14⁰

UP

Bfst.
10⁰ x 10⁰

SNACK BAR

P.

Kit
10⁰ x 12⁰

R.

DN

Gar.
19⁴ x 25⁴

E.

Din.
13⁴ x 11⁰

COVERED PORCH

40' - 0"

44' - 8"

© design basics inc.

135

Features

- Traditional elevation combines aesthetics and economy.
- Symmetrical coat closets and cased openings frame view to great room and entry.
- Versatile dining room has parlor option.
- Bayed dinette with back yard access and staircase to second level.
- Deluxe laundry room and built-in bookcase

provide ample amenities to fantastic upper level.
- Luxurious master suite contains built-in dresser between his and her walk-in closets.
- Roomy compartmented dressing area with whirlpool.
- Extra storage in deep garage.

First Floor	852 sq. ft.
Second Floor	893 sq. ft.
Total Living Area	1,745 sq. ft.

PRICE CODE: C

136

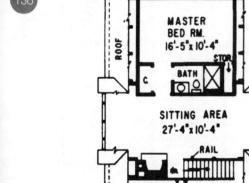

SECOND FLOOR

MASTER BED RM.
16'-5"x 10'-4"

BATH

STOR.

SITTING AREA
27'-4"x 10'-4"

RAIL

RAIL

OPEN

ROOF

ROOF

C.

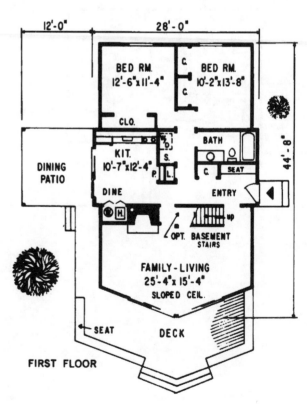

FIRST FLOOR

12'-0"   28'-0"

BED RM.
12'-6"x 11'-4"

C.

BED RM.
10'-2"x 13'-8"

C.

CLO.

DINING PATIO

KIT.
10'-7"x 12'-4"

W.
S.
P. L.

BATH

SEAT

C.

DINE

ENTRY

OPT. BASEMENT STAIRS

up

FAMILY-LIVING
25'-4"x 15'-4"
SLOPED CEIL.

44'-8"

SEAT

DECK

First Floor	1,126 sq. ft.
Second Floor	624 sq. ft.
Total Living Area	1,750 sq. ft.

PRICE CODE: B

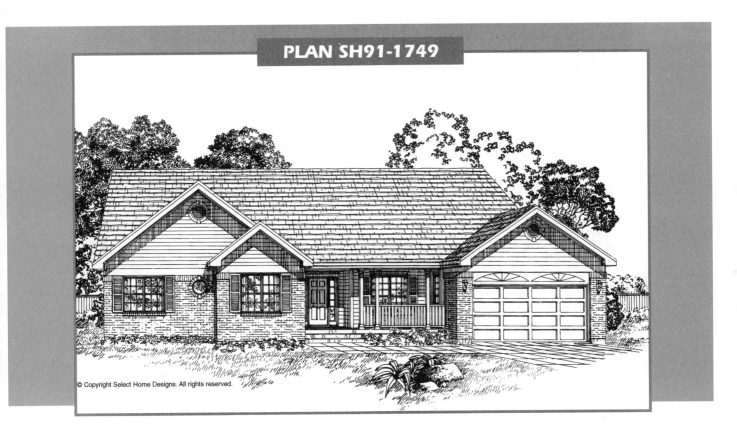

PLAN SH91-1749

Exterior view of Rear Elevation

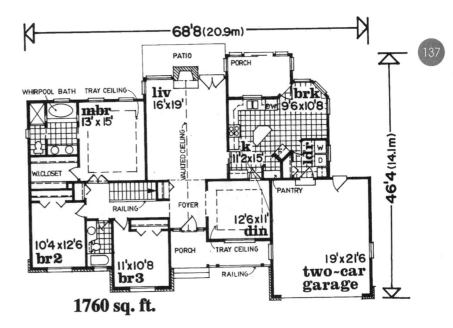

137

1760 sq. ft.

Features

- Covered, railed porch provides a weather-protected entry and introduces the vaulted foyer.
- Vaulted ceiling, extending from the foyer through to the living room, increases the sense of spaciousness.
- Floor plan is designed for a home with a view to the rear of the lot.
- Tray ceiling adds distinction and creates a formal atmosphere for the dining room.

- Open kitchen includes a walk-in pantry, centre preparation island and breakfast bay.
- Windows surrounding the sunroom capture the sun's heat and warm this area.
- Master bedroom boasts a tray ceiling, walk-in closet and lavish ensuite with twin vanity, whirlpool spa and private lavish shower.

Total Living Area: 1,760 sq. ft.

PRICE CODE: B

CUSTOMIZE IT!

ORDER TOLL FREE   1 ■ 800 ■ 533 ■ 4350   24-HOUR FAX ORDERING   1 ■ 800 ■ 344 ■ 4293

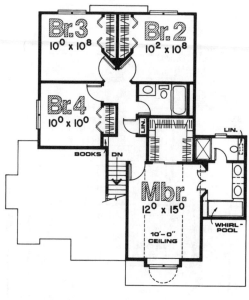

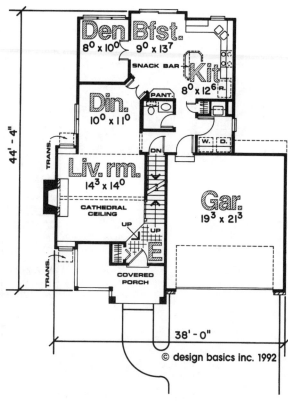

© design basics inc. 1992

Features

- This simple but charming design presents a well-balanced elevation for narrow lots.
- From entry, step down into volume living room open to formal dining area for expanded entertaining flexibility.
- Double doors access formal dining room from kitchen.
- Open kitchen/dinette features large pantry, center island with snack bar and corner sink.
- Private den may be converted to sunroom.
- Laundry room conveniently located off dinette.
- Master suite includes volume ceilings, walk-in closet, dual lavs and whirlpool tub.

First Floor	869 sq. ft.
Second Floor	895 sq. ft.
Total Living Area	1,764 sq. ft.

PRICE CODE: C

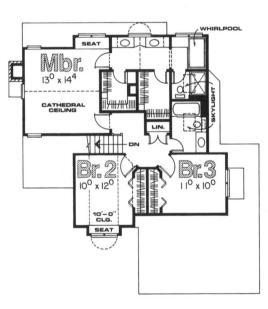

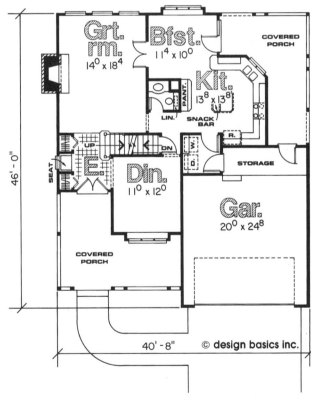

139

Features

- Covered porch and Victorian accents create this classical elevation.
- Double doors to entry open to spacious great room and elegant dining room.
- Gourmet kitchen features island/snack bar and large pantry.
- French doors lead to breakfast area with access to covered porch and kitchen.

- Cathedral ceilings in master bedroom and dressing area add an exquisite touch.
- His and her walk-in closets, large dressing area with dual lavs and whirlpool complement master bedroom.
- Vaulted ceiling in bedroom #2 accents window seat and arched transom window.

First Floor	**905 sq. ft.**
Second Floor	**863 sq. ft.**
Total Living Area	**1,768 sq. ft.**

PRICE CODE: C

BEDROOM #2
10'-0" x 14'-7"

BATH 2
SKYLIGHT

BEDROOM #3
12'-0" x 14'-7"

DN.

OPEN TO LIVING ROOM BELOW

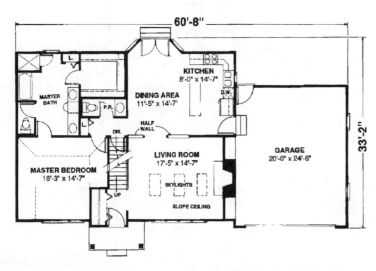

60'-8"

KITCHEN
8'-0" x 14'-7"

MASTER BATH

DINING AREA
11'-5" x 14'-7"

D.W.

P.R.

HALF WALL

33'-2"

DN.

LIVING ROOM
17'-5" x 14'-7"

GARAGE
20'-0" x 24'-6"

MASTER BEDROOM
16'-3" x 14'-7"

SKYLIGHTS

UP

SLOPE CEILING

Lillibrook Cottage

Features

- Compact design with contemporary amenities.
- Appealing gable roof design.
- Columned entry porch adds to the attractiveness of this home.
- Entry porch leads directly into sky lighted living room with fireplace.
- Dining room at rear features French doors and L-shaped kitchen.
- Left wing includes large master bedroom with deluxe master bath and walk-in closet.
- Upstairs, two additional bedrooms share a uniquely designed bath.

First Floor	**1,220 sq. ft.**
Second Floor	**630 sq. ft.**
Total Living Area	**1,850 sq. ft.**

PRICE CODE: B

PLAN DB2308

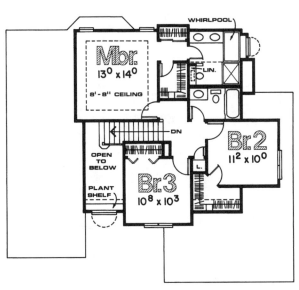

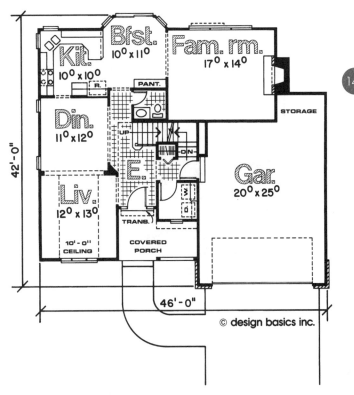

141

© design basics inc.

Features

- Sleek lines, covered porch and window details enhance elevation.
- Volume entry views bright living room with adjoining dining room.
- Kitchen enjoys gourmet features and bayed dinette.
- Family room enhanced by window-brightened wall and raised-hearth fireplace.
- Garage includes extra storage space.

- Bedroom #2 includes huge walk-in closet.
- Secondary bedrooms convenient to bath.
- Hall design affords seclusion to luxurious master suite with boxed ceiling.
- Pampering master bath/dressing area includes two closets, whirlpool with plant sill and double lavs.

First Floor	1,032 sq. ft.
Second Floor	743 sq. ft.
Total Living Area	1,775 sq. ft.

PRICE CODE: C

CUSTOMIZE IT!

ORDER TOLL FREE 1■800■533■4350   24-HOUR FAX ORDERING 1■800■344■4293

142

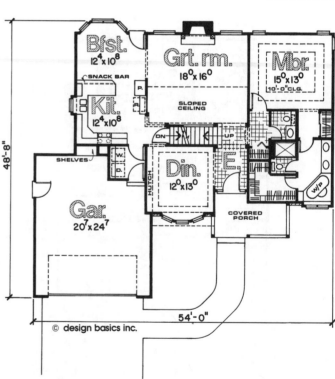

© design basics inc.

Features

- Inviting covered porch.
- Elegant bayed window in formal dining room off entry.
- Beautiful fireplace with windows showcased in large great room.
- Bright bayed dinette.
- Kitchen with window above sink, pantry and snack bar.

- Utility entrance through garage.
- Additional storage in garage.
- Master suite features tiered ceiling, corner windows and luxurious dressing area with double lav vanity, 2 closets and corner whirlpool under windows.
- Convenient hall bath services secondary bedrooms.

First Floor	**1,348 sq. ft.**
Second Floor	**430 sq. ft.**
Total Living Area	**1,778 sq. ft.**

PRICE CODE: C

CUSTOMIZE IT!

ORDER TOLL FREE 1■800■533■4350   **24-HOUR FAX ORDERING** 1■800■344■4293

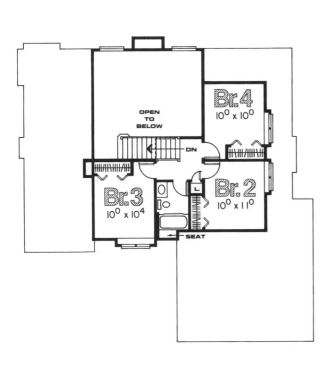

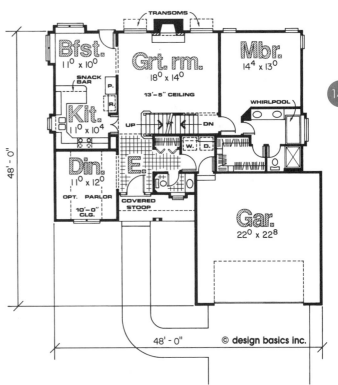

143

Features

- Versatile dining room off entry has 10-foot volume ceiling and parlor option.
- French doors at base of stairs create an elegant passage to peninsula kitchen with snack bar.
- Corner boxed windows create sunny and inviting breakfast area.
- Volume ceiling allows staircase to overlook great room.
- Secluded master suite features dual lavs, whirlpool bath and generous walk-in closet.
- Upstairs, 3 secondary bedrooms share hall bath with seat at tub.

First Floor	**1,265 sq. ft.**
Second Floor	**518 sq. ft.**
Total Living Area	**1,783 sq. ft.**

PRICE CODE: C

PLAN JA5149

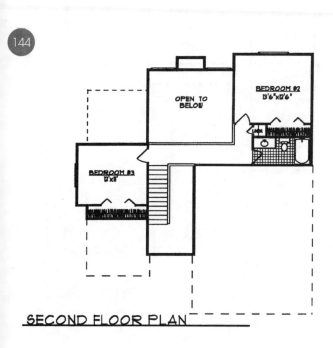

SECOND FLOOR PLAN

BEDROOM #2
13'6"x12'6"

OPEN TO BELOW

BEDROOM #3
12'x11'

MAIN FLOOR PLAN

NOOK
10'x9'6"

GREAT ROOM
14'9"x17'6"

MASTER BEDROOM
13'6"x14'6"

KITCHEN
12'x11'6"

DINING ROOM
10'x12'6"

FOYER

2 CAR GARAGE
20'x22'

45'0"

42'0"

144

First Floor	1,250 sq. ft.
Second Floor	534 sq. ft.
Total Living Area	1,784 sq. ft.

PRICE CODE: B

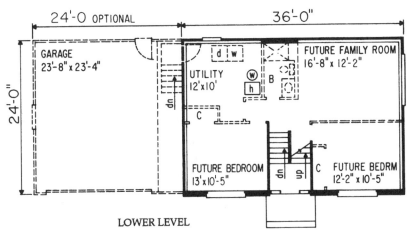

24'-0 OPTIONAL

36'-0"

GARAGE
23'-8" x 23'-4"

d w

UTILITY
12'x10'

FUTURE FAMILY ROOM
16'-8" x 12'-2"

W
h
B

C

dn

24'-0"

up

FUTURE BEDROOM
13'x10'-5"

dn

C

FUTURE BEDRM
12'-2" x 10'-5"

LOWER LEVEL

145

deck

dn.

BEDROOM
9'-10" x 11'

C

B

L

DINING
9' x 10'

KITCHEN
8' x 10'

C

26'-0"

C

rail

**MASTER
BEDROOM**
13'-4" x 11'-6"

dn

up

LIVING ROOM
14'-10" x 15'

MAIN LEVEL

Expansion
Bi-Level

Features

- This is the perfect home for those willing to add to their dream home.
- Main floor can be built with future expansion possible in lower level.
- Combined living and dining areas are located on the right.
- Master bedroom and second bedroom occupy the left side.

First Floor	923 sq. ft.
Second Floor	876 sq. ft.
Total Living Area	1,799 sq. ft.

PRICE CODE: B

PLAN AM2140

146

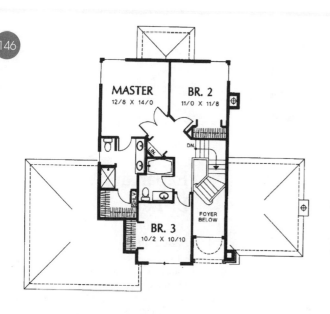

MASTER 12/8 X 14/0

BR. 2 11/0 X 11/8

DN.

BR. 3 10/2 X 10/10

FOYER BELOW

◄ 52' ►

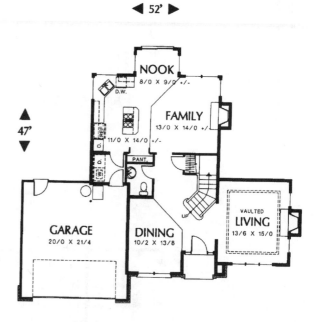

47'

NOOK 8/0 X 9/0 +/-

D.W.

FAMILY 13/0 X 14/0 +/-

11/0 X 14/0 +/-

REF.

W. D.

PANT.

UP

GARAGE 20/0 X 21/4

DINING 10/2 X 13/8

VAULTED LIVING 13/6 X 15/0

First Floor	1,050 sq. ft.
Second Floor	750 sq. ft.
Total Living Area	1,800 sq. ft.

PRICE CODE: B

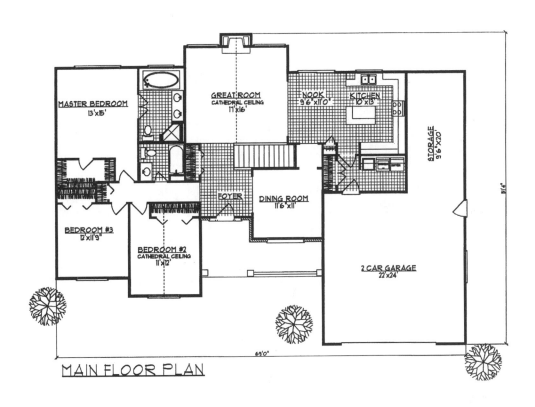

MASTER BEDROOM
13'x15'

GREAT ROOM
CATHEDRAL CEILING
11'x16'

NOOK
9'6"x11'0"

KITCHEN
10'x13'

STORAGE
9'6"x20'

BEDROOM #3
12'x11'9"

FOYER

DINING ROOM
11'6"x11'

BEDROOM #2
CATHEDRAL CEILING
11'x12'

2 CAR GARAGE
22'x24'

69'0"

MAIN FLOOR PLAN

Total Living Area   1,802 sq. ft.

PRICE CODE: B

CUSTOMIZE IT!

ORDER TOLL FREE   1■800■533■4350   24-HOUR FAX ORDERING   1■800■344■4293

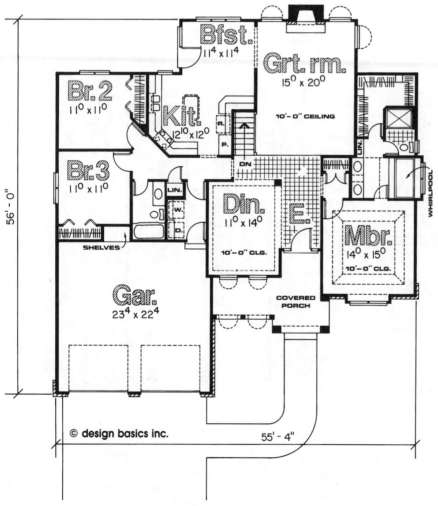

148

Bfst.
$11^4 \times 11^4$

Grt. rm.
$15^0 \times 20^0$
10'-0" CEILING

Br. 2
$11^0 \times 11^0$

Kit.
$12^{10} \times 12^0$

Br. 3
$11^0 \times 11^0$

Dln.
$11^0 \times 14^0$
10'-0" CLG.

Mbr.
$14^0 \times 15^0$
10'-0" CLG.

WHIRLPOOL

DN

R.

P.

LIN.

LIN.

W.

D.

SHELVES

Gar.
$23^4 \times 22^4$

COVERED PORCH

56'-0"

55'-4"

© design basics inc.

Features

- Beautiful columns and arched transoms are focal points of this ranch home elevation.
- 10-foot entry has formal views of volume dining room and great room featuring brick fireplace and arched windows.
- Large island kitchen offers angled range and pantry.
- Sunny breakfast room has atrium door to back yard.
- Garage with built-in shelves accesses home through efficient laundry room.
- Separate bedroom wings provide optimum privacy.
- Private master suite includes whirlpool bath with sloped ceiling, plant shelf above dual lavs and large walk-in closet.

Total Living Area   1,806 sq. ft.

PRICE CODE: C

CUSTOMIZE IT!

ORDER TOLL FREE   1▪800▪533▪4350   24-HOUR FAX ORDERING   1▪800▪344▪4293

149

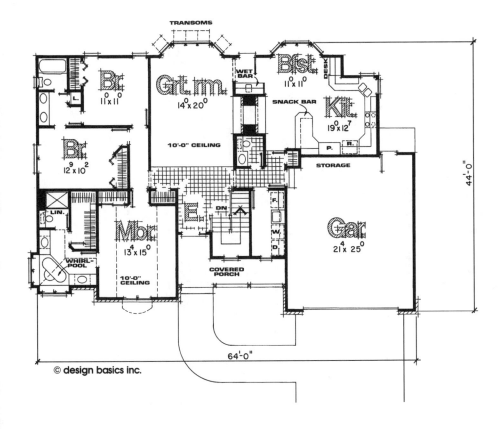

© design basics inc.

TRANSOMS

Br.
11 x 11

Br.
12 x 10

Grt. rm.
14⁰ x 20⁰

10'-0" CEILING

WET BAR

Bfst.
11⁰ x 11⁰

SNACK BAR

Kit.
19⁰ x 12⁷

DESK

P.   R.

STORAGE

Mbr.
13⁴ x 15⁰

10'-0" CEILING

WHIRL-POOL

LIN.

DN

F.

W.

D.

Gar.
21⁰ x 25⁰

COVERED PORCH

44'-0"

64'-0"

Features

- Front porch features repeating arches.
- Hard-surfaced traffic ways.
- 10-foot ceilings through entry, great room and staircase.
- Sunny dinette with planning desk and bayed window.
- Roomy kitchen with pantry, 2 lazy Susans and snack bar shares see-thru fireplace with great room.
- Wet bar/servery between dinette and great room.
- Oversized garage with plenty of storage.
- Volume master bedroom with arched window.
- Master bath has walk-in closet, his and her vanities and corner whirlpool tub with windows above.
- Hollywood bath for secondary bedrooms.

Total Living Area   1,808 sq. ft.

PRICE CODE: C

CUSTOMIZE IT!

ORDER TOLL FREE   1▪800▪533▪4350   24-HOUR FAX ORDERING   1▪800▪344▪4293

PLAN FD8081A

150

Total Living Area   1,812 sq. ft.

151

Total Living Area   1,812 sq. ft.

PRICE CODE: B

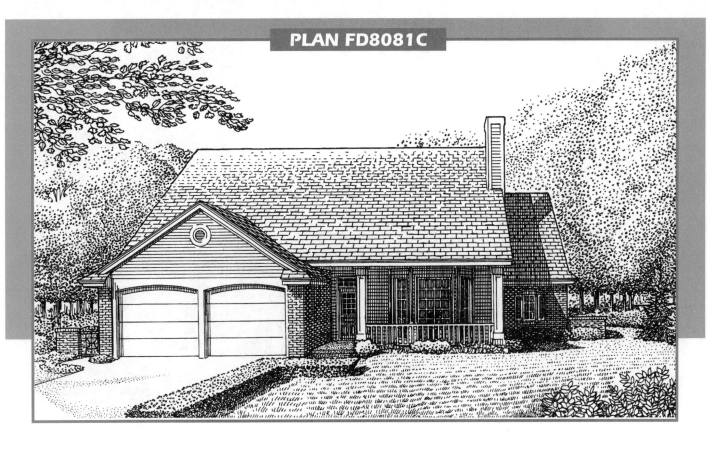

50'-0"

62'-2"

Bed#3
11x11
8'-0" Clg.

Brkfst
11x11
9'-0" Clg.

Covered
Patio

Sitting
Area
8'-0" Clg.

Bed#2
11x11
8'-0" Clg.

Kit
11x11
9'-0" Clg.

FmlDin
10x10
10'-0" Clg.

MstrBed
14x19
9'-0" Vaulted Clg.

Bed#4
11x10
8'-0" Clg.

Ent
10'-0" Clg.

LivRm
16x19
Cathedral Clg.

Util

Walk-In
Closet

Cov
Por

Gar
19x21

© Copyright Fillmore Design Group

Total Living Area   1,812 sq. ft.

PLAN AM2113A

◀ 36' ▶

153

▲
33'
▼

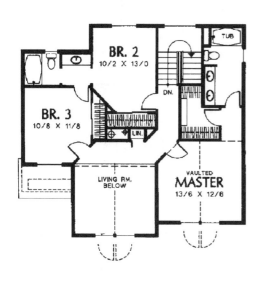

BR. 2
10/2 X 13/0

TUB

DN.

BR. 3
10/8 X 11/8

LIN.

LIVING RM. BELOW

VAULTED
MASTER
13/6 X 12/6

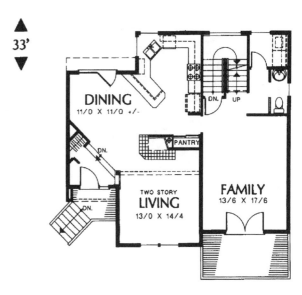

DINING
11/0 X 11/0 +/-

DN. UP

DN.

PANTRY

TWO STORY
LIVING
13/0 X 14/4

FAMILY
13/6 X 17/6

DN.

TWO CAR GARAGE BELOW

First Floor	1,022 sq. ft.
Second Floor	813 sq. ft.
Total Living Area	1,835 sq. ft.

PRICE CODE: B

CUSTOMIZE IT!

ORDER TOLL FREE 1■800■533■4350   24-HOUR FAX ORDERING 1■800■344■4293

PLAN DB2547

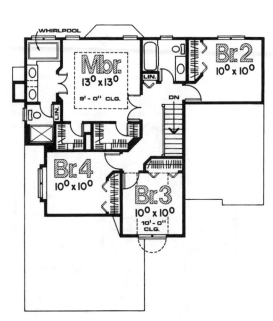

WHIRLPOOL

Mbr.
13⁰ x 13⁰
9'-0" CLG.

Br. 2
10⁰ x 10⁰

LIN.

DN

LIN.

Br. 4
10⁰ x 10⁰

Br. 3
10⁰ x 10⁰
10'-0" CLG.

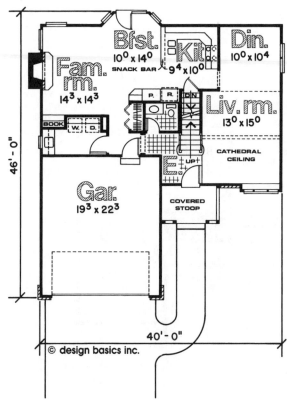

46'-0"

Bfst.
10⁰ x 14⁰
SNACK BAR

Kit.
9⁴ x 10⁰

Din.
10⁰ x 10⁴

Fam.
rm.
14³ x 14³

Liv. rm.
13⁰ x 15⁰

BOOK

W. D.

P. R.

DN

UP

CATHEDRAL
CEILING

Gar.
19³ x 22³

COVERED
STOOP

40'-0"

© design basics inc.

Features

- Attractive 2-story home with brick accenting front elevation.
- Handsome wood floor joins the family room, dinette and kitchen.
- Family room is highlighted by a fireplace and useful built-in bookcase.
- Dinette is a bright point featuring delightful bayed windows.

- Formal entertaining options multiply as dining room opens to volume living room.
- Impressive double doors lead to a distinctive master bedroom distinguished by his and her walk-in closets.
- French doors open to luxurious master bath featuring dual vanities, large whirlpool and separate shower area.

First Floor	964 sq. ft.
Second Floor	877 sq. ft.
Total Living Area	1,841 sq. ft.

PRICE CODE: C

CUSTOMIZE IT!

ORDER TOLL FREE 1■800■533■4350   24-HOUR FAX ORDERING 1■800■344■4293

PLAN DB1752

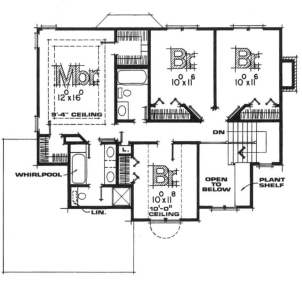

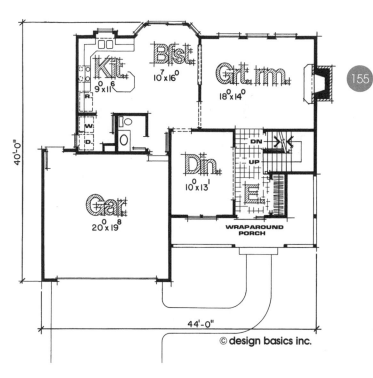

155

© design basics inc.

Features

- 2-story entry with large coat closet and plant shelf above.
- Strategically located staircase.
- Great room with many windows.
- Island kitchen with boxed window over sink.
- Large bayed dinette.
- Convenient powder bath location.
- Main floor laundry.

- Volume ceiling and arched window in front bedroom.
- Pleasant secondary bedrooms with interesting angles.
- Large master suite with his and her walk-in closets, corner windows and bath area featuring double vanity and whirlpool bath.

First Floor	919 sq. ft.
Second Floor	927 sq. ft.
Total Living Area	1,846 sq. ft.

PRICE CODE: C

CUSTOMIZE IT!

ORDER TOLL FREE 1■800■533■4350   24-HOUR FAX ORDERING 1■800■344■4293

PLAN DB2950

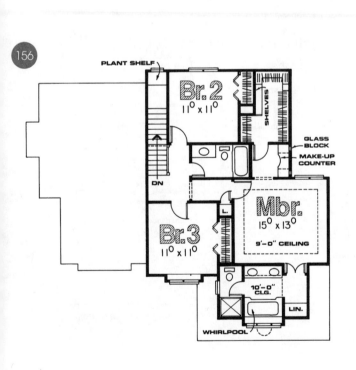

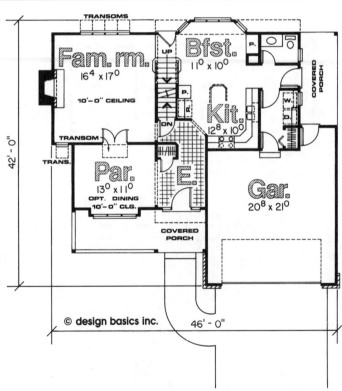

© design basics inc.

Features

- Parlor off entry has dining room option and French doors to family room.
- Back yard door shared by large family room and bayed breakfast area with pantry.
- Island kitchen open to breakfast area features a second pantry and 2 lazy Susans.
- Desirable mud porch allows side yard access to utility area with 1/2 bath and laundry room.
- Back stairs lead to well-planned second level.
- Secondary bedrooms share hall bath.
- Amenities abound in master suite with whirlpool bath, built-in linen cabinet and ample walk-in closet off dressing area.

First Floor	972 sq. ft.
Second Floor	877 sq. ft.
Total Living Area	**1,849 sq. ft.**

PRICE CODE: C

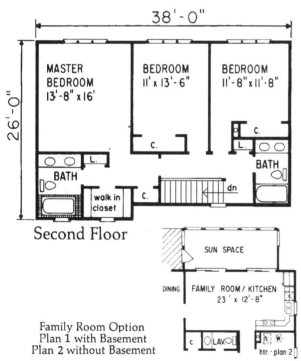

Second Floor

38'-0"

26'-0"

MASTER BEDROOM
13'-8" x 16'

BEDROOM
11' x 13'-6"

BEDROOM
11'-8" x 11'-8"

c.

c.

L.

BATH

L.

walk in closet

BATH

dn

SUN SPACE

DINING

FAMILY ROOM / KITCHEN
23' x 12'-8"

c.   LAV.

htr. - plan 2

Family Room Option
Plan 1 with Basement
Plan 2 without Basement

First Floor

42'-0"

8'-0"

24'-0"

53'-8"

DECK

SUN SPACE

DINING RM
11'-7" x 12'-8"

KITCHEN
11'-8" x 12'-8"

LIVING ROOM
13'-8" x 23'-4"

c.   LAV.

htr. - plan 2

FOYER

up   dn

W.   D.

PORCH

GARAGE
21'-4" x 21'-4"

157

Stylish Colonial Haven

Features

- Foyer opens to large L-shaped living room/dining room.
- Two sliding glass doors provide access to rear sun space from the dining room and L-shaped kitchen.
- Access the rear deck from either the sun room or living room.

- Second floor features a master bedroom with walk-in closet and full bath with double vanity.
- Bedrooms upstairs are served by a full bath with double vanity. Sun space, 160 square feet.

First Floor	**912 sq. ft.**
Second Floor	**940 sq. ft.**
Sun Space	**160 sq. ft.**
Total Living Area	**2,012 sq. ft.**

PRICE CODE: B

PLAN DB2236

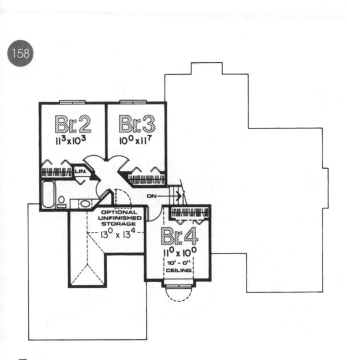

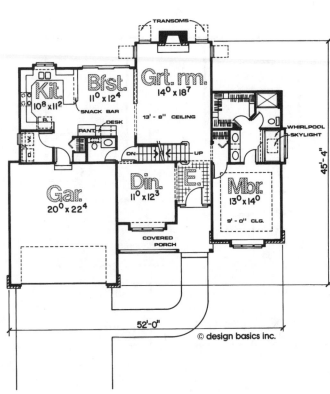

Features

- Inviting covered front porch.
- Formal dining room with large boxed window seen from entry.
- Views into great room reveal handsome fireplace and tall windows.
- Snack bar, pantry, 2 lazy Susans and desk for kitchen/dinette area.
- Closet at service entry through garage.

- Window in laundry room.
- Large boxed window in volume master bedroom.
- Skylit master dressing area with double vanity, whirlpool, compartmented stool and shower.
- Upstairs, fourth bedroom has volume ceiling above beautiful arched window.

First Floor	1,297 sq. ft.
Second Floor	558 sq. ft.
Total Living Area	1,855 sq. ft.

PRICE CODE: C

PLAN NP1335

MASTER BEDROOM
14'-4" x 16'-4"

BEDROOM
11'-1" x 14'-0"

BEDROOM
12'-0" x 11'-10"

BATH 1

BATH 2

LINEN

DN.

Second Floor

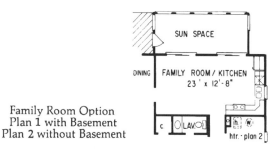

SUN SPACE

DINING

FAMILY ROOM / KITCHEN
23' x 12'-8"

LAV

c

htr. - plan 2

Family Room Option
Plan 1 with Basement
Plan 2 without Basement

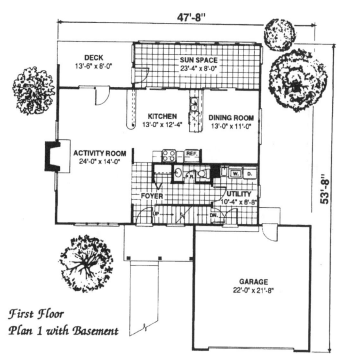

47'-8"

DECK
13'-6" x 8'-0"

SUN SPACE
23'-4" x 8'-0"

KITCHEN
13'-0" x 12'-4"

DINING ROOM
13'-0" x 11'-0"

ACTIVITY ROOM
24'-0" x 14'-0"

REF.

W.   D.

FOYER

UTILITY
10'-4" x 8'-8"

UP

DN.

GARAGE
22'-0" x 21'-8"

53'-8"

First Floor
Plan 1 with Basement

159

Sunshine Manor

Features

- Traditional Colonial design with special, contemporary touches.
- Tiled entry foyer opens to staircase and large activity room with fireplace.
- Powder room, entry closet, and utility area conveniently located near entrance.
- Tiled sun space room has sliding door access to both the kitchen and dining room.
- Upstairs features three comfortable bedrooms and two full baths.
- Sun space, 160 square feet.

First Floor	912 sq. ft.
Second Floor	940 sq. ft.
Sun Space	192 sq. ft.
Total Living Area	2,044 sq. ft.

PRICE CODE: B

PLAN AM2135A

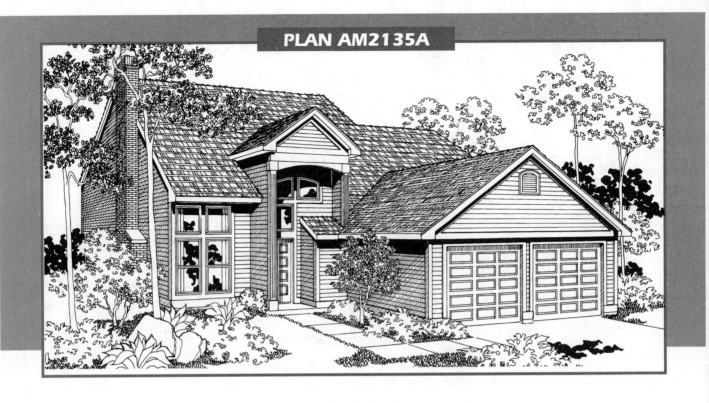

◄ 40' ►

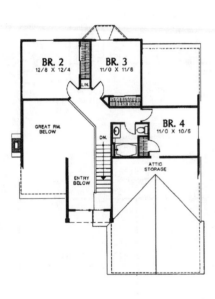

▲
53'
▼

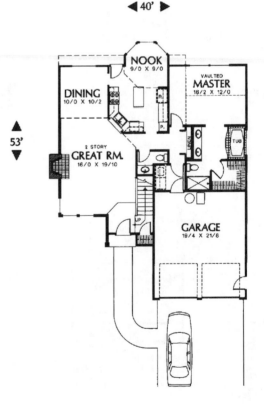

First Floor   1,230 sq. ft.
Second Floor   636 sq. ft.
Total Living Area   1,866 sq. ft.

PRICE CODE: B

PLAN DB1330

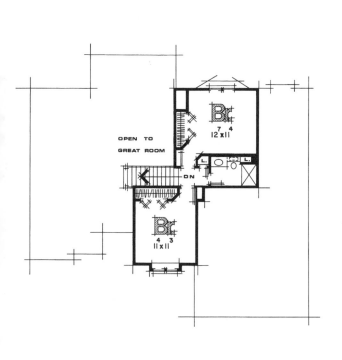

OPEN TO GREAT ROOM

Br.
12 x 11

Br.
11 x 11

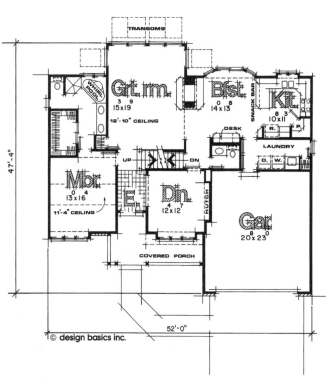

TRANSOMS

Grt. rm.
15 x 19
12'-10" CEILING

Bfst.
14 x 13

Kit.
10 x 11

WHIRL POOL

DESK

LAUNDRY

Mbr.
13 x 16
11'-4" CEILING

UP   DN

Din.
12 x 12

HUTCH

D. W.

Gar.
20 x 23

COVERED PORCH

47'-4"

52'-0"

© design basics inc.

Features

- Entry open to formal dining room with hutch space.
- Volume great room with see-thru fireplace flooded with natural light from large windows to the back.
- Hearth kitchen area with bayed dinette, has see-thru fireplace, planning desk and large corner walk-in pantry.
- Conveniently located powder bath.

- Main floor mud/laundry area with coat closet and laundry sink.
- Centralized bathroom convenient for secondary bedrooms.
- Master suite with sloped ceiling includes walk-in closet, double vanity and corner whirlpool tub.

First Floor	1,421 sq. ft.
Second Floor	448 sq. ft.
Total Living Area	1,869 sq. ft.

PRICE CODE: C

PLAN NPT109

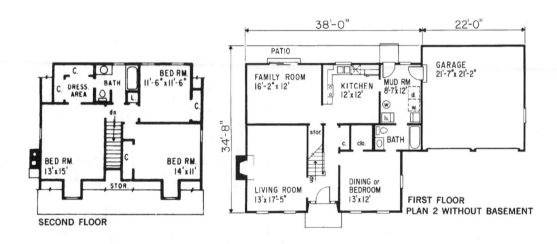

SECOND FLOOR

BED RM. 11'-6"x11'-6"

DRESS. AREA

BATH

BED RM. 13'x15'

BED RM. 14'x11'

STOR.

38'-0"

22'-0"

PATIO

FAMILY ROOM 16'-2" x 12'

KITCHEN 12'x12'

MUD RM 8'-7"x12'

GARAGE 21'-7"x 21'-2"

34'-8"

stor.

BATH

LIVING ROOM 13'x17'-5"

DINING or BEDROOM 13'x12'

FIRST FLOOR PLAN 2 WITHOUT BASEMENT

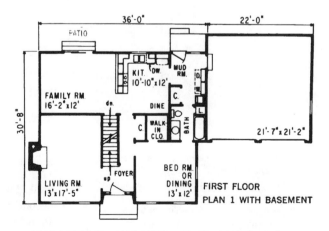

36'-0"

22'-0"

PATIO

KIT. 10'-10"x12'

MUD RM.

FAMILY RM. 16'-2" x12'

DINE

30'-8"

WALK-IN CLO.

BATH

21'-7"x 21'-2"

LIVING RM. 13'x17'-5"

FOYER

BED RM. OR DINING 13'x12'

FIRST FLOOR PLAN 1 WITH BASEMENT

PLEASE SPECIFY PLAN 1 OR 2 WHEN ORDERING BLUEPRINT PLAN

First Floor	1,068 sq. ft.
Second Floor	804 sq. ft.
Total Living Area	1,872 sq. ft.

PRICE CODE: B

C U S T O M I Z E   I T !

ORDER TOLL FREE 1■800■533■4350 **24-HOUR FAX ORDERING** 1■800■344■4293

PLAN NP CASCADE

163

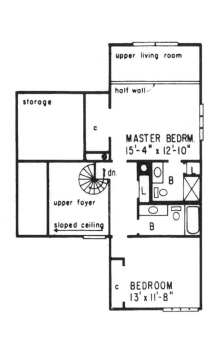

upper living room

half wall

storage

c

MASTER BEDRM.
15'-4" x 12'-10"

dn.

upper foyer

B

sloped ceiling

B

L

c BEDROOM
13' x 11'-8"

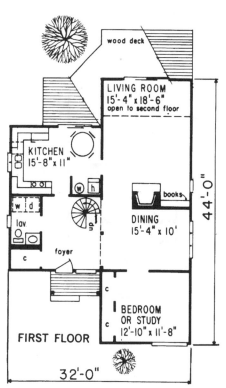

wood deck

LIVING ROOM
15'-4" x 18'-6"
open to second floor

KITCHEN
15'-8" x 11"

w   h

books

w   d

DINING
15'-4" x 10'

lav.

up

foyer

c

44'-0"

c

BEDROOM
OR STUDY
12'-10" x 11'-8"

c

FIRST FLOOR

32'-0"

First Floor	1,088 sq. ft.
Second Floor	784 sq. ft.
Total Living Area	1,872 sq. ft.

PRICE CODE: B

SECOND FLOOR

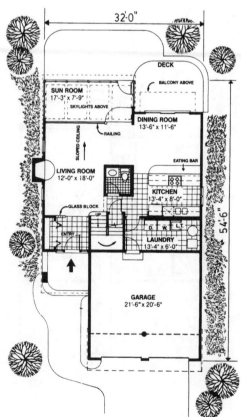

Hidden Treasures

Features

- Perfect for a narrow lot.
- Spacious, comfortable design.
- Sloped ceilings crown entry and living room.
- Dining room adjoins kitchen with breakfast bar.
- Sunken sun room with skylights is delightful retreat or perfect for entertaining.

- Optional multi-level wooden deck can be accessed either from sun room or dining room.
- Two bedrooms with bath and master bedroom with private bath upstairs.
- Balcony off master bedroom overlooks living room.

First Floor	896 sq. ft.
Second Floor	977 sq. ft.
Total Living Area	1,873 sq. ft.

PRICE CODE: B

CUSTOMIZE IT!

ORDER TOLL FREE 1■800■533■4350   **24-HOUR FAX ORDERING** 1■800■344■4293

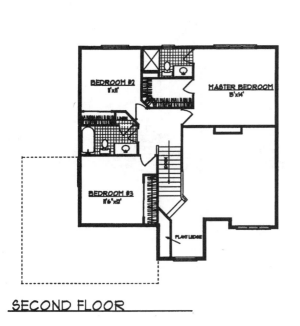

SECOND FLOOR

MAIN FLOOR PLAN

First Floor	1,080 sq. ft.
Second Floor	794 sq. ft.
Total Living Area	1,874 sq. ft.

PRICE CODE: B

SKYLIGHTS

Br.
12⁰x11⁰

Mbr.
14 x 13

CATHEDRAL
CEILING

CLOTHES
CHUTE

DN

OPEN TO
BELOW

Br.
11 x 12

10'-0"CLG.

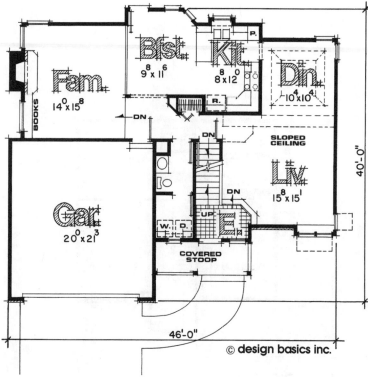

Fam.
14⁰x15⁸

Bfst.
9⁸x11

Kit.
8⁰x12

Din.
10⁴x10⁴

BOOKS

DN

DN

SLOPED
CEILING

Liv.
15⁸x15¹

Gar.
20⁰x21³

DN

UP

W. D.

COVERED
STOOP

40'-0"

46'-0"

© design basics inc.

Features

- Covered front porch.
- Step-down from entry into volume living room open to formal dining room with vaulted ceiling.
- Window in compartmented main-floor laundry area.
- Awning window centers above bookcase in family room with fireplace.

- Well-planned kitchen with lazy Susan, pantry and many cabinets is open to breakfast area.
- Cathedral ceiling in master bedroom.
- Skylit dressing area and compartmented stool in master bath, plus walk-in closet.
- Volume ceiling in front bedroom with beautiful arched window.

First Floor	1,042 sq. ft.
Second Floor	833 sq. ft.
Total Living Area	1,875 sq. ft.

PRICE CODE: C

CUSTOMIZE IT!

ORDER TOLL FREE   1▪800▪533▪4350   24-HOUR FAX ORDERING   1▪800▪344▪4293

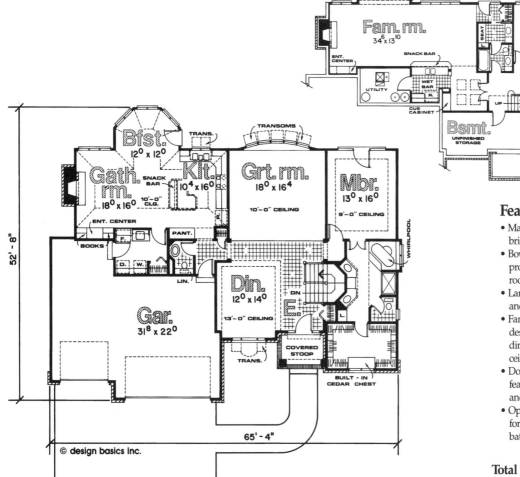

GAME AREA
$11^7 \times 7^4$

Fam. rm.
$34^6 \times 13^{10}$

SEAT

Br. 2
$13^6 \times 11^0$

ENT. CENTER

SNACK BAR

WET BAR R.

UTILITY

CUE CABINET

UP

Br. 3
$12^6 \times 11^0$

Bsmt.
UNFINISHED STORAGE

OPTIONAL BASEMENT

Bfst.
$12^0 \times 12^0$

TRANS.

TRANSOMS

Gath. rm.
$18^0 \times 16^0$
$10'-0''$ CLG.

Kit.
$10^4 \times 16^0$

SNACK BAR

Grt. rm.
$18^0 \times 16^4$
$10'-0''$ CEILING

Mbr.
$13^0 \times 16^0$
$9'-0''$ CEILING

ENT. CENTER

BOOKS

F.

PANT.

D. W.

LIN.

Din.
$12^0 \times 14^0$
$13'-0''$ CEILING

DN

WHIRLPOOL

Gar.
$31^8 \times 22^0$

COVERED STOOP

TRANS.

BUILT-IN CEDAR CHEST

52' - 8"

65' - 4"

© design basics inc.

Features

- Majestic window highlights handsome brick front elevation.
- Bowed windows and high ceiling provide terrific airy feeling to great room.
- Large laundry accessible from kitchen and garage.
- Family living is highlighted in integrated design of gathering room, spacious dinette and kitchen, all with special ceiling treatments.
- Double doors into master dressing area featuring angled lavs, make-up counter and huge walk-in closet with cedar chest.
- Optional finished basement designed for independent living, with kitchen, bath and private access.

Total Living Area   **1,887 sq. ft.**

PRICE CODE: C

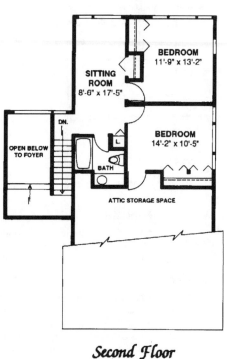

Second Floor

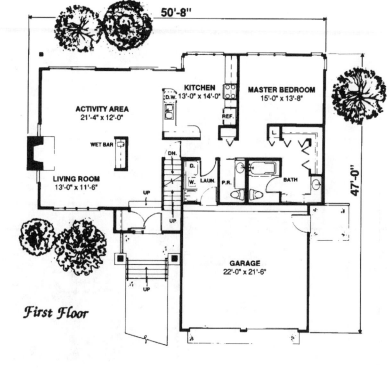

First Floor

Heritage Crest

Features

- Pillared, walk-up front porch showcases front entrance door with circle top window and sidelight.
- Enter a open, high-ceiling foyer with direct access to large living room with fireplace.
- Living room/activity area features an open design with wet bar.
- Large kitchen off activity area.
- First-floor master bedroom includes dressing area and private bath.
- Second floor balcony open to foyer, with sitting room for study or relaxation and two large bedrooms with full bath.

First Floor	1,337 sq. ft.
Second Floor	643 sq. ft.
Total Living Area	1,980 sq. ft.

PRICE CODE: B

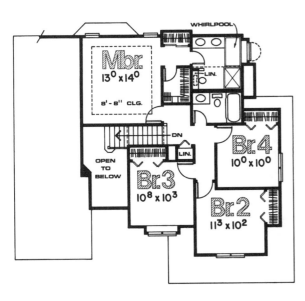

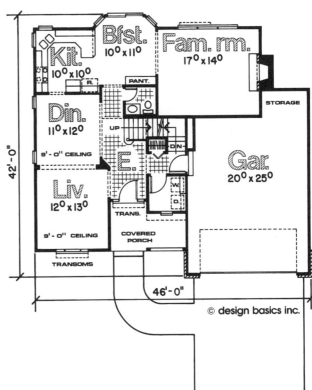

169

© design basics inc.

Features

- Elegant lines of this two-story elevation give additional enticement.
- Dramatic tiled entry hall leads conveniently to all areas.
- Adjacent living and dining areas enhance every entertaining pursuit.
- Kitchen and bayed breakfast area located strategically to serve both the formal dining area and the family room.
- Bright picture window and lovely raised hearth fireplace highlight family room.
- Second level arrangement offers unique privacy to secondary bedrooms and gives seclusion to master suite.
- Sumptuous master suite features two closets and a sunlit whirlpool tub and dressing area.

First Floor	1,032 sq. ft.
Second Floor	865 sq. ft.
Total Living Area	1,897 sq. ft.

PRICE CODE: C

PLAN AM2130B

170

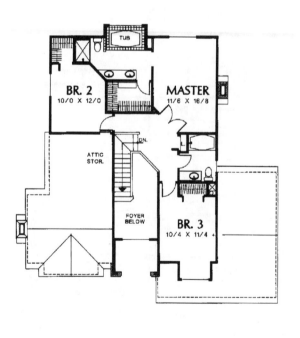

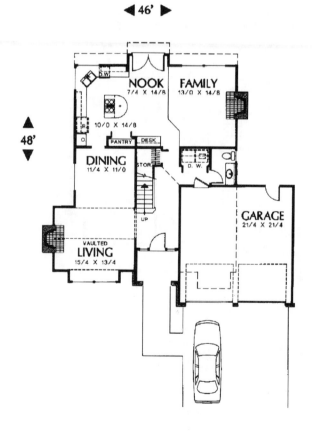

◀ 46' ▶

▲
48'
▼

First Floor	1,062 sq. ft.
Second Floor	838 sq. ft.
Total Living Area	1,900 sq. ft.

PRICE CODE: B

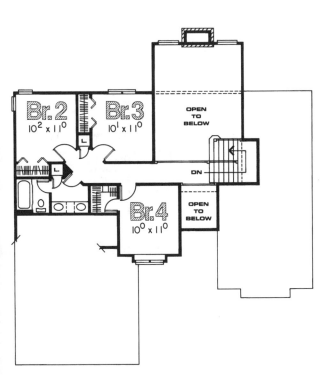

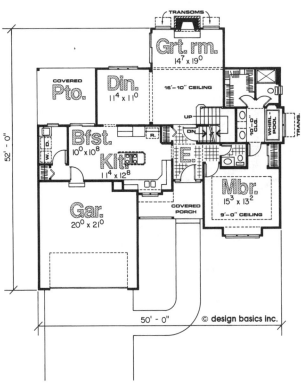

171

Features

- Sleek lines coupled with impressive detailing enhance elevation.
- Entry opens into volume great room with fireplace flanked by cheerful windows.
- Dining room off great room offers entertaining options.
- Kitchen and breakfast area has cooktop in island and access to covered patio.

- Bridge overlook on second level.
- Secondary bedrooms share compartmented bath with dual lavs.
- Master bedroom secluded on first level includes decorative ceiling and bright boxed window.
- Luxurious master bath has two closets, separate wet and dry areas, dual lavs and whirlpool tub.

First Floor	**1,302 sq. ft.**
Second Floor	**599 sq. ft.**
Total Living Area	**1,901 sq. ft.**

PRICE CODE: C

172

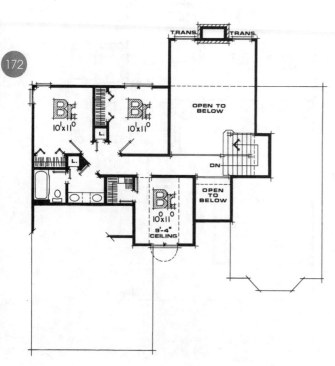

TRANS. TRANS.

OPEN TO BELOW

Br.
10'x11⁰

Br.
10'x11⁰

L.

DN

Br.
10⁰x11

OPEN TO BELOW

9'-4"
CEILING

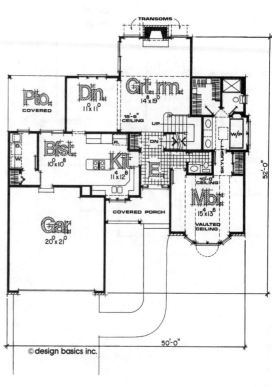

TRANSOMS

Pto.
COVERED

Din.
11'x11⁰

Grt. rm.
14'x19⁰

15'-8"
CEILING

UP

Bfst.
10'x10⁸

Kit.
11'x12⁸

DN

W/P

SKYLIGHT

10'-0"
CEILING

Gar.
20⁰x21⁰

COVERED PORCH

Mbr.
15'x13⁶

VAULTED
CEILING

52'-0"

50'-0"

© design basics inc.

Features

- Volume hard-surfaced entry with coat closet.
- Volume ceiling in great room with fireplace flanked by windows.
- Dining room open to great room for expanded entertaining.
- Island kitchen adjoins breakfast area with access to covered patio.
- Laundry room with sink, closet and window to the back.
- Upstairs landing overlooks entry and great room below.
- Master bedroom with volume ceiling and arched bayed window adjoins luxury skylit dressing/bath area with whirlpool, walk-in closet and plant shelf.
- Secondary bedrooms share generous compartmented bath.

First Floor	1,306 sq. ft.
Second Floor	599 sq. ft.
Total Living Area	1,905 sq. ft.

PRICE CODE: C

CUSTOMIZE IT!

PLAN NP1324

173

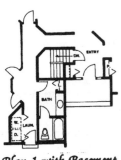

Plan 1 with Basement

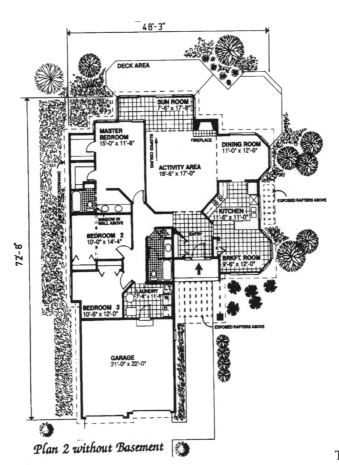

Plan 2 without Basement

Eastwind

Features

- Handsome, contemporary design marks this home as special.
- Entry foyer opens to kitchen and breakfast area on the right and a large activity area area on the left,
- Activity area amenities include a fireplace and sun room.
- Formal dining area with bay windows and sliding glass doors located at rear of kitchen.
- Master bedroom has his/her walk-in closets and a dual- vanity bath.
- Two additional bedrooms share one full bath.

Total Living Area　　1,907 sq. ft.

PRICE CODE: B

174

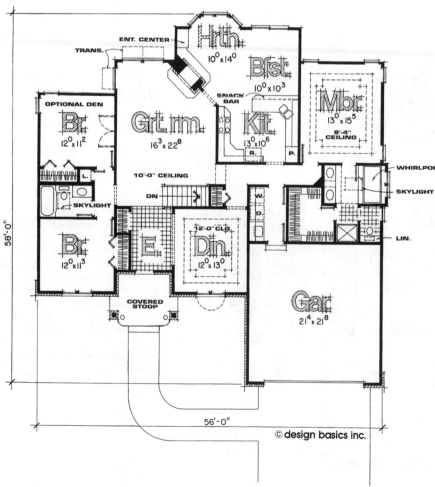

TRANS.

ENT. CENTER

Hrth.
10⁰ x 14⁰

Bfst.
10⁰ x 10³

OPTIONAL DEN

Br
12⁰ x 11²

Grt. rm.
16³ x 22⁸

SNACK BAR

Kit.
13⁰ x 10⁶

Mbr
13⁰ x 15⁵
9'-4" CEILING

R.

P.

WHIRLPOOL

SKYLIGHT

10'-0" CEILING

SKYLIGHT

DN

L.

W.

D.

LIN.

Br
12⁰ x 11³

E.

Dn.
12⁰ x 13⁰
12'-0" CLG.

Gar.
21⁴ x 21⁸

COVERED STOOP

58'-0"

56'-0"

© design basics inc.

Features

- Alternate elevation at no extra cost.
- 10-foot ceiling at entry and great room.
- Beautiful arched dining room window and detailed ceiling to 12 foot high.
- See-thru fireplace seen from entry.
- Hearth area open to kitchen.
- Gourmet kitchen caters to the serious cook with corner sink, pantry, snack bar and adjacent eating area.
- Add French doors to bedroom adjacent to great room for optional den, remove closet for built-in bookcase.
- Master bedroom with vaulted ceiling and corner windows.
- Complete master bath area with skylight, whirlpool, his and her vanity and large walk-in closet.

Total Living Area   1,911 sq. ft.

PRICE CODE: C

PLAN AM2106D

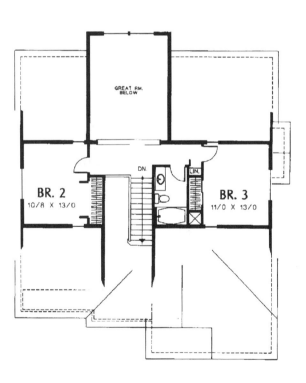

GREAT RM. BELOW.

BR. 2
10/8 X 13/0

DN.

LIN.

BR. 3
11/0 X 13/0

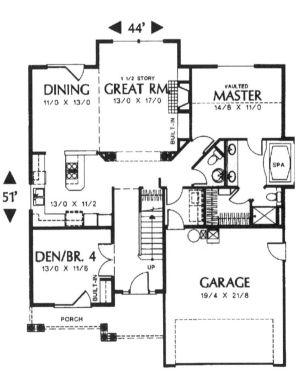

◀ 44' ▶

DINING
11/0 X 13/0

1 1/2 STORY
GREAT RM
13/0 X 17/0

VAULTED
MASTER
14/8 X 11/0

BUILT-IN

SPA

▲
51'
▼

13/0 X 11/2

DEN/BR. 4
13/0 X 11/6

BUILT-IN

UP

GARAGE
19/4 X 21/8

PORCH

First Floor	1,396 sq. ft.
Second Floor	523 sq. ft.
Total Living Area	1,919 sq. ft.

PRICE CODE: B

CUSTOMIZE IT!

ORDER TOLL FREE **1▪800▪533▪4350** 24-HOUR FAX ORDERING **1▪800▪344▪4293**

PLAN DB2551

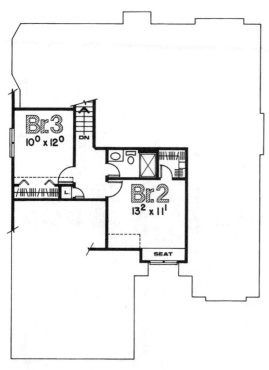

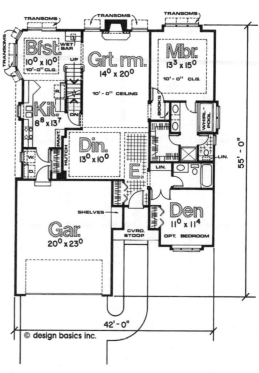

© design basics inc.

Features

- Convenient for a private home office, French doors off entry reveal an optional den.
- Staircase to second level is conveniently located at back of house, off of kitchen.
- Lofty, open great room features raised hearth fireplace flanked by 2 large windows.
- Wet bar placed for easy access from great room and dinette.

- Extensive windows and volume ceiling make dinette bright.
- Seclusion is optimized in well-appointed master suite.
- Second level front bedroom has delightful window seat and ample walk-in closet.

First Floor	1,486 sq. ft.
Second Floor	441 sq. ft.
Total Living Area	1,927 sq. ft.

PRICE CODE: C

177

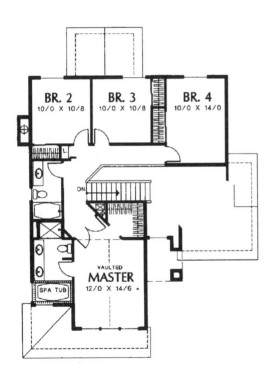

BR. 2
10/0 X 10/8

BR. 3
10/0 X 10/8

BR. 4
10/0 X 14/0

DN

VAULTED
MASTER
12/0 X 14/6 +

SPA TUB

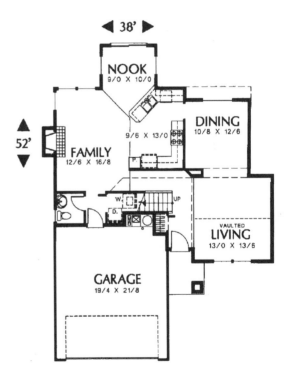

◀ 38' ▶

NOOK
9/0 X 10/0

52'

FAMILY
12/6 X 16/8

9/6 X 13/0

DINING
10/8 X 12/6

W.

D.

UP

VAULTED
LIVING
13/0 X 13/6

GARAGE
19/4 X 21/8

First Floor	960 sq. ft.
Second Floor	968 sq. ft.
Total Living Area	1,928 sq. ft.

PRICE CODE: B

178

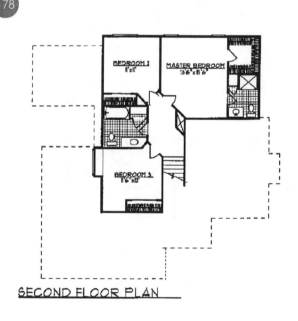

SECOND FLOOR PLAN

FIRST FLOOR PLAN

First Floor	1,132 sq. ft.
Second Floor	797 sq. ft.
Total Living Area	1,929 sq. ft.

PRICE CODE: B

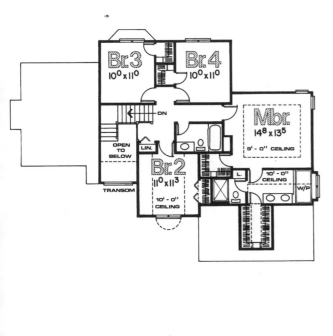

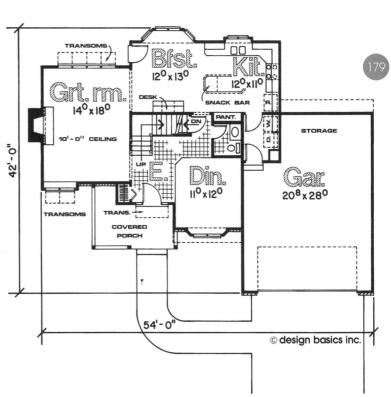

© design basics inc.

Features

- Inviting covered porch.
- Interesting staircase with landing in volume entry.
- Abundant windows throughout.
- 10-foot ceiling and handsome fireplace in great room.
- Island counter, pantry and desk in open kitchen/dinette area.

- Kitchen conveniently accesses laundry room.
- Upstairs landing overlooks entry below.
- Beautiful arched window under volume ceiling in bedroom #2.
- Master suite features pampering dressing area with double vanity, compartmented stool and shower plus whirlpool under window.

First Floor	944 sq. ft.
Second Floor	987 sq. ft.
Total Living Area	1,931 sq. ft.

PRICE CODE: C

CUSTOMIZE IT!

PLAN MN1941

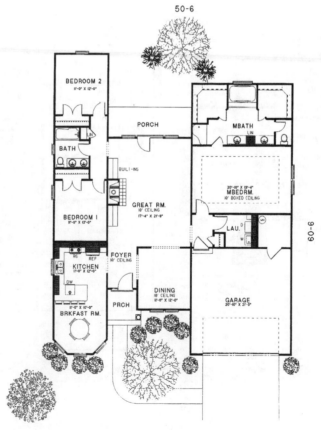

50-6

60-9

BEDROOM 2
11'-0" X 12'-0"

PORCH

MBATH
LIN

BATH

BUILT-INS

20'-10" X 13'-4"
MBEDRM.
10' BOXED CEILING

GREAT RM.
10' CEILING
17'-4" X 21'-8"

BEDROOM 1
11'-0" X 12'-0"

LAU D
W

RG   REF

KITCHEN
11'-0" X 12'-0"

FOYER
10' CEILING

DW

DINING
10' CEILING
11'-0" X 12'-0"

GARAGE
20'-10" X 21'-0"

PRCH

BRKFAST RM.

180

Total Living Area   1,941 sq. ft.

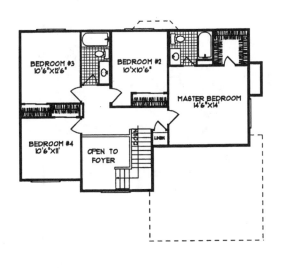

SECOND FLOOR PLAN

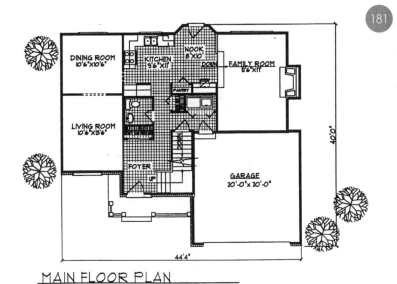

MAIN FLOOR PLAN

181

First Floor	992 sq. ft.
Second Floor	950 sq. ft.
Total Living Area	1,942 sq. ft.

PRICE CODE: B

PLAN DB2554

OPEN TO
GREAT ROOM

Br. 3
11³ x 13⁷

LIN.

DN

Br. 4
11⁰ x 11⁰
10'-0" CEILING

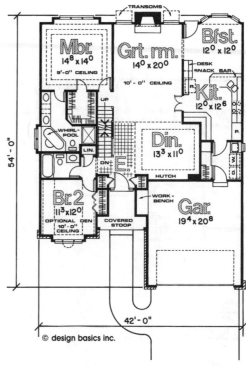

TRANSOMS

Mbr.
14⁸ x 14⁰
9'-0" CEILING

Grt. rm.
14⁰ x 20⁰
10'-0" CEILING

Bfst.
12⁰ x 12⁰

DESK
SNACK BAR

UP

WHIRL-
POOL

LIN.

Kit.
12⁰ x 12⁶

Din.
13³ x 11⁰

DN

HUTCH

Br. 2
11³ x 12⁰
OPTIONAL DEN
10'-0" CEILING

COVERED
STOOP

WORK-
BENCH

Gar.
19⁴ x 20⁸

54'-0"

42'-0"

© design basics inc.

Features

- Rhythmic use of arches creates a notable elevation.
- Practical use of space is demonstrated by the placement of 2 closets in the entry.
- Optional den is accentuated by dramatic windows and a dramatic ceiling.
- Lofty open great room features a fireplace flanked by large windows.
- Dinette featuring a desk and snack bar also

provides convenient access to the outdoors.
- Garage features built-in workbench.
- Master suite features a deluxe bath with whirlpool and dual lavs and large walk-in closet.
- Second level front bedroom achieves a feeling of spaciousness with a 10-foot ceiling and arch-top window.

First Floor	1,517 sq. ft.
Second Floor	431 sq. ft.
Total Living Area	1,948 sq. ft.

PRICE CODE: C

CUSTOMIZE IT!

ORDER TOLL FREE 1 ■ 800 ■ 533 ■ 4350   24-HOUR FAX ORDERING   1 ■ 800 ■ 344 ■ 4293

SECOND FLOOR

walk-in clo.

BATH

BATH

BEDROOM
12'-8" x 12'-4"

C

MASTER
BEDROOM
13' x 15'

dn.

C

BEDROOM
15' x 11'-6"

roof

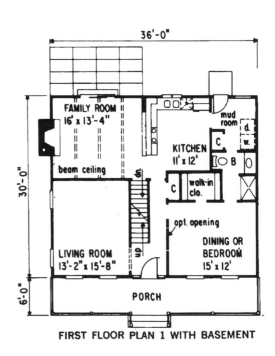

FIRST FLOOR PLAN 1 WITH BASEMENT

36'-0"

30'-0"

6'-0"

FAMILY ROOM
16' x 13'-4"

beam ceiling

mud room

d.
w.

KITCHEN
11' x 12'

C

B

walk-in clo.

C

opt. opening

LIVING ROOM
13'-2" x 15'-8"

up

DINING OR
BEDROOM
15' x 12'

PORCH

First Floor	1,080 sq. ft.
Second Floor	868 sq. ft.
Total Living Area	1,948 sq. ft.

PRICE CODE: B

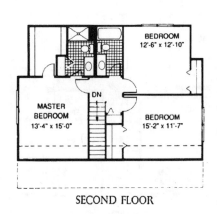

SECOND FLOOR

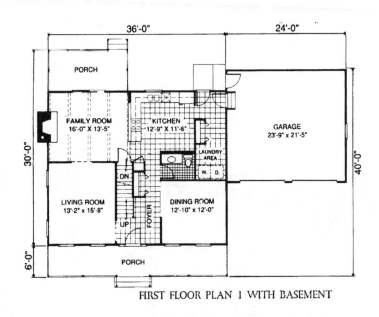

FIRST FLOOR PLAN 1 WITH BASEMENT

Down-Home Delight

Features

- Nothing could be sweeter than to view this home as yours.
- Beautiful, front-spanning porch exudes warmth.
- Living room and dining room flank the entrance hall.
- Cozy family room features beamed ceiling and fireplace.
- L-shaped kitchen roomy enough for small dining table.
- Upstairs, master bedroom has generous walk-in closet and private bath.
- Two additional upstairs bedrooms are served by full bath.

First Floor	1,080 sq. ft.
Second Floor	868 sq. ft.
Total Living Area	1,948 sq. ft.

PRICE CODE: B

CUSTOMIZE IT!

ORDER TOLL FREE 1∙800∙533∙4350   24-HOUR FAX ORDERING 1∙800∙344∙4293

PLAN DB2384

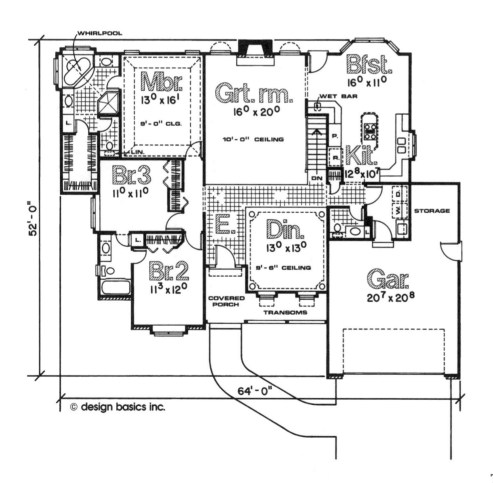

WHIRLPOOL

Mbr.
13⁰ x 16¹
9'-0" CLG.

Grt. rm.
16⁰ x 20⁰
10'-0" CEILING

Bfst.
16⁰ x 11⁰

WET BAR

Kit.
12⁸ x 10⁷

Br.3
11⁰ x 11⁰

Din.
13⁰ x 13⁰
9'-6" CEILING

Br.2
11³ x 12⁰

STORAGE

Gar.
20⁷ x 20⁸

COVERED PORCH

TRANSOMS

52'-0"

64'-0"

Features

- Wood and brick details and elegant porch highlight elevation.
- Entry with 10-foot ceiling views open dining room with tapered columns.
- Gourmet kitchen includes island, pantry and wrapping wet bar/servery.
- Sunny bayed dinette with outdoor access.
- Great room enjoys a warm fireplace flanked by large windows with arched transoms above.
- Elegant master suite enjoys vaulted ceilings, pampering master bath with his and her vanities, whirlpool, linen cabinet, special shower and roomy walk-in closet.
- Garage includes extra storage space and door to side yard.

Total Living Area   1,948 sq. ft.

PRICE CODE: C

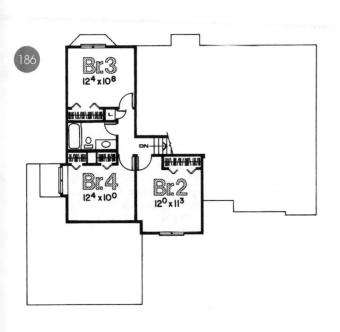

186

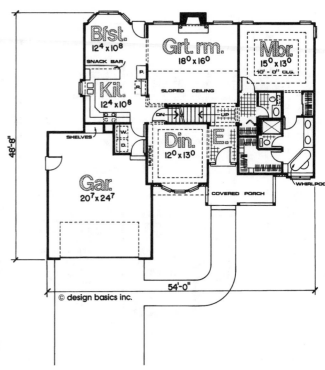

© design basics inc.

Features

- Quaint covered porch formal dining room with elegant bayed window seen from entry.
- Large windows flank handsome fireplace in great room.
- Tiered ceiling and corner windows in master bedroom.

- Pampering master dressing/bath area features two closets, double vanity and angled whirlpool in corner under window.
- 3 bedrooms on second level served by hall bath.

First Floor	**1,348 sq. ft.**
Second Floor	**603 sq. ft.**
Total Living Area	**1,951 sq. ft.**

PRICE CODE: C

CUSTOMIZE IT!

ORDER TOLL FREE 1 ▪ 800 ▪ 533 ▪ 4350   24-HOUR FAX ORDERING   1 ▪ 800 ▪ 344 ▪ 4293

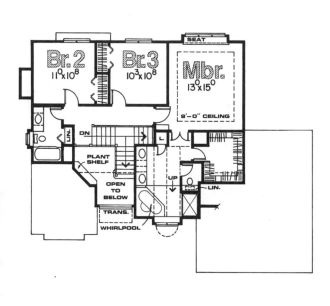

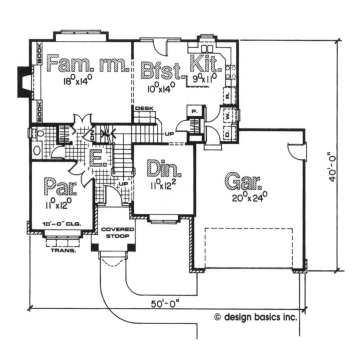

© design basics inc.

Features

- Brilliant design character captures great livability in this striking 2-story home.
- Whether used as office, library, or as formal living room, parlor with privacy is valuable design.
- T-shaped staircase smooths traffic flow.
- Well-appointed kitchen is just steps away from dinette and dining room.

- Integrated design of family room, dinette and kitchen capitalize on comfortable family living and easy entertaining.
- Charming window seat complements comfortable master bedroom.
- All desired amenities such as walk-in closet, dual lavs and whirlpool are featured in master bath.

First Floor	**1,082 sq. ft.**
Second Floor	**869 sq. ft.**
Total Living Area	**1,951 sq. ft.**

PRICE CODE: C

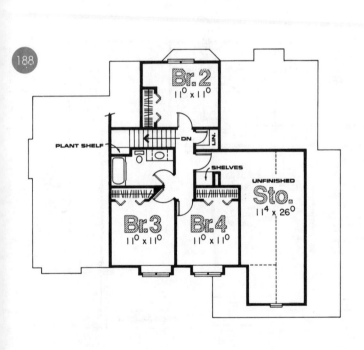

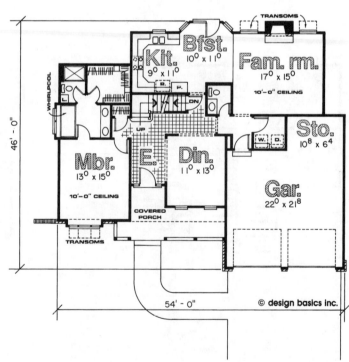

Features

- Country style elevation highlighted by detailed porch and brick accents.
- Well-integrated family room, kitchen and breakfast area accommodate many family activities.
- Master suite contains 10-foot-high ceilings while angled doors in the whirlpool bath add drama.
- 3 secondary bedrooms share roomy hall bath serviced by large linen.
- Ample unfinished storage is a great feature in this 1 1/2 story home.

First Floor	**1,348 sq. ft.**
Second Floor	**609 sq. ft.**
Total Living Area	**1,957 sq. ft.**

PRICE CODE: C

PLAN AM2152A

◀ 40' ▶

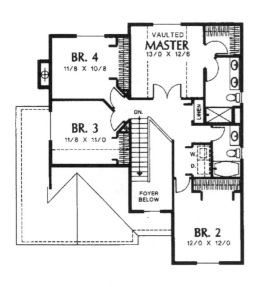

BR. 4
11/8 X 10/8

VAULTED
MASTER
13/0 X 12/6

LINEN

DN.

BR. 3
11/8 X 11/0

W.

D.

FOYER
BELOW

BR. 2
12/0 X 12/0

42'

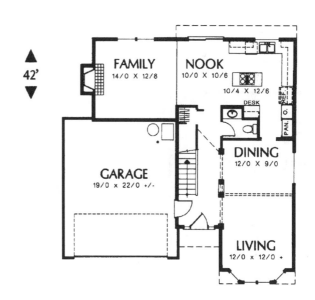

FAMILY
14/0 X 12/8

NOOK
10/0 X 10/6

10/4 X 12/6

DESK

PAN. | O. | REF.

GARAGE
19/0 x 22/0 +/-

DINING
12/0 X 9/0

LIVING
12/0 x 12/0 +

First Floor	944 sq. ft.
Second Floor	1,013 sq. ft.
Total Living Area	1,957 sq. ft.

PRICE CODE: B

PLAN AM2155A

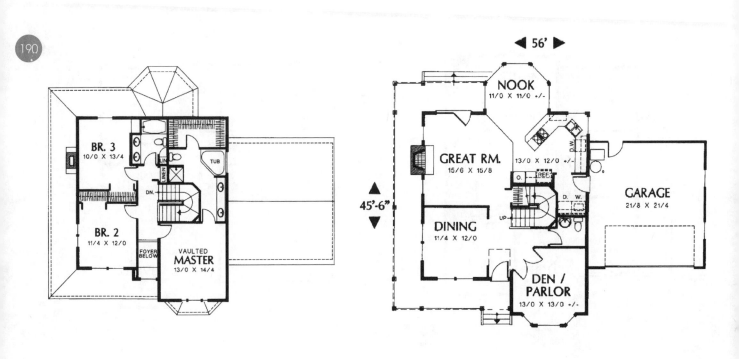

BR. 3
10/0 X 13/4

BR. 2
11/4 X 12/0

LINEN

DN.

TUB

FOYER
BELOW

VAULTED
MASTER
13/0 X 14/4

◀ 56' ▶

NOOK
11/0 X 11/0 +/-

GREAT RM.
15/6 X 15/8

DINING
11/4 X 12/0

45'-6"

UP

D. W.

GARAGE
21/8 X 21/4

DEN /
PARLOR
13/0 X 13/0 +/-

First Floor	1,060 sq. ft.
Second Floor	898 sq. ft.
Total Living Area	1,958 sq. ft.

PRICE CODE: B

PLAN MN1963

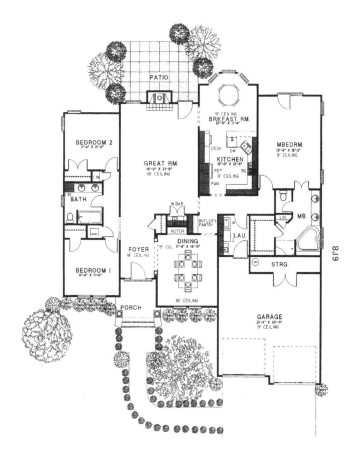

Total Living Area   1,963 sq. ft.

PRICE CODE: B

192

SECOND FLOOR

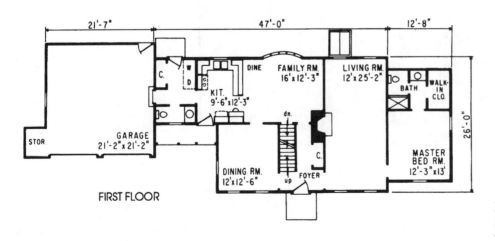

FIRST FLOOR

Colonial Fair

Features

- Colonial grace with practical application.
- Secluded master bedroom suite offers full bath and walk-in closet on first floor.
- Formal dining room and kitchen with informal dining area adjacent to spacious family room.
- Long living room features fireplace on interior wall.
- Service entry into the kitchen eliminates messy traffic from main entry.
- Two large upstairs bedrooms with full bath perfect for children.

First Floor	1,337 sq. ft.
Second Floor	636 sq. ft.
Total Living Area	1,973 sq. ft.

PRICE CODE: B

193

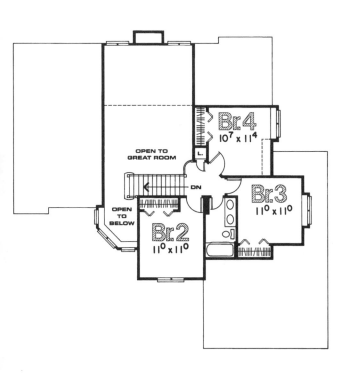

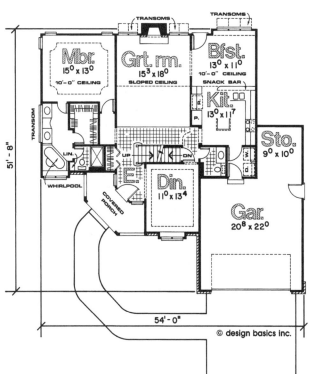

© design basics inc.

Features

- Angled porch, with wood railing, and shutter treatments inspire country mood.
- Majestic great room beckons with high ceiling and sunny, tall windows framing fireplace.
- Well-designed kitchen offers daily cooking ease while bright dinette has exit to outdoors.

- Spacious master bath features angled whirlpool, dual lavs, shower and spacious walk-in closet.
- Three bedrooms and bath complete livable upper level.
- Large storage space in garage area helps maximize full usage of home.

First Floor	1,413 sq. ft.
Second Floor	563 sq. ft.
Total Living Area	1,976 sq. ft.

PRICE CODE: C

CUSTOMIZE IT!

ORDER TOLL FREE **1■800■533■4350**   24-HOUR FAX ORDERING   **1■800■344■4293**

194

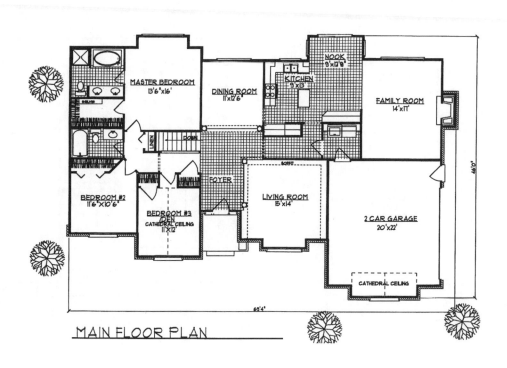

MASTER BEDROOM
13'6"x16'

DINING ROOM
11'x12'6"

KITCHEN
9'x13'

NOOK
9'x12'9"

FAMILY ROOM
14'x17'

LINEN

DOWN

FOYER

LIVING ROOM
15'x14'

BEDROOM #2
11'6"x10'6"

BEDROOM #3
DEN
CATHEDRAL CEILING
11'x12'

2 CAR GARAGE
20'x22'

CATHEDRAL CEILING

46'0"

62'4"

MAIN FLOOR PLAN

Total Living Area   1,984 sq. ft.

PRICE CODE: B

PLAN JA5529

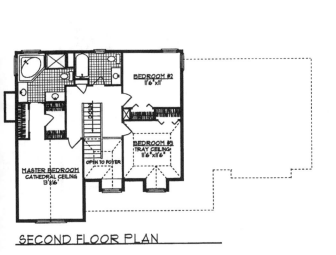

SECOND FLOOR PLAN

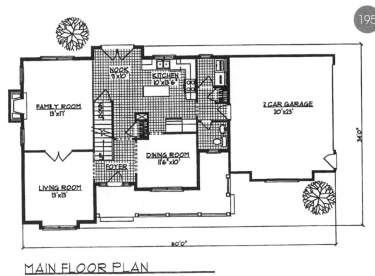

MAIN FLOOR PLAN

First Floor	1,065 sq. ft.
Second Floor	921 sq. ft.
Total Living Area	1,986 sq. ft.

PRICE CODE: B

PLAN DB852

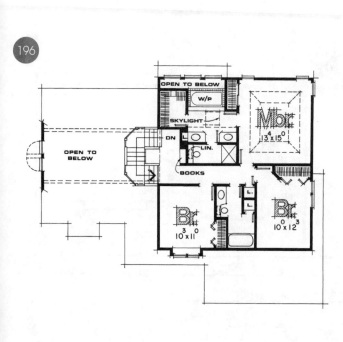

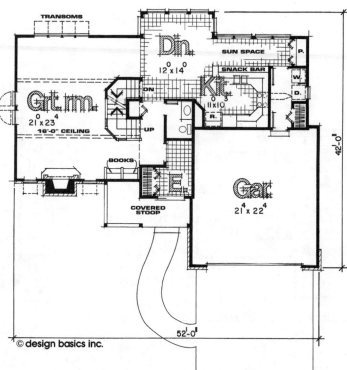

© design basics inc.

Features

- Energy efficient airlock entry with coat closet.
- Wrapping staircase open to spacious volume great room with bookcases, fireplace and large windows to the back.
- Phone booth at base of staircase.
- Gourmet kitchen includes 2 lazy Susans, pantry and snack bar to serve adjacent sun space and dining area.

- Garage accesses home through laundry/mud room with coat closet and iron-a-way.
- Master suite features vaulted ceiling, 2 closets, his and her vanities and whirlpool tub.
- Secondary bedrooms share hall bath served by 2 linen closets.

First Floor	1,108 sq. ft.
Second Floor	879 sq. ft.
Total Living Area	1,987 sq. ft.

PRICE CODE: C

PLAN MN1987

197

Total Living Area   1,987 sq. ft.

PRICE CODE: B

198

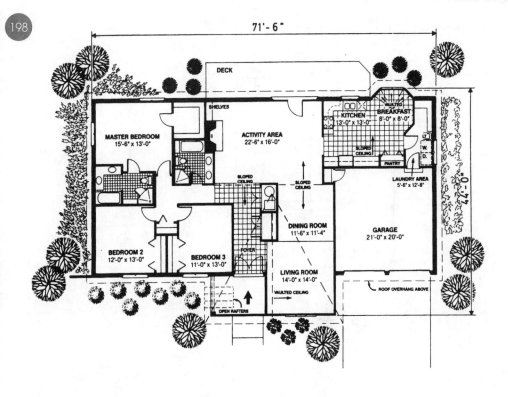

71'- 6 "

DECK

SHELVES

MASTER BEDROOM
15'-6" x 13'-0"

ACTIVITY AREA
22'-6" x 16'-0"

KITCHEN
13'-0" x 13'-0"

VAULTED
BREAKFAST
8'-0" x 8'-0"

SLOPED
CEILING

PANTRY

W.
D.

LAUNDRY AREA
5'-6" x 12'-8"

SLOPED
CEILING

SLOPED
CEILING

DINING ROOM
11'-6" x 11'-4"

GARAGE
21'-0" x 20'-0"

BEDROOM 2
12'-0" x 13'-0"

BEDROOM 3
11'-0" x 13'-0"

FOYER

LIVING ROOM
14'-0" x 14'-0"

VAULTED CEILING

ROOF OVERHANG ABOVE

OPEN RAFTERS

Ranch Castille

Features

- A practical design with an attractive, arched main entrance mark this home as something special.
- Left wing includes master bedroom with walk-in closet and bathroom suite.
- Two additional bedroom in the left wing share a full bath with both tub and shower.
- Right wing features a living room with vaulted ceiling, and a dining room and activity room with sloped ceilings for added interest.
- Kitchen is tucked away at the left rear and includes sloped ceiling and built-in pantry.
- Vaulted breakfast nook includes bay window.
- Large deck off activity area for expanding your entertaining options.

Total Living Area **1,990 sq. ft.**

PRICE CODE: B

PLAN DB2315

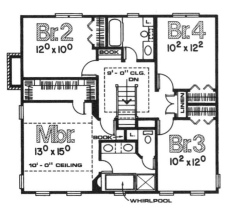

Br. 2
12⁰ x 10⁰

Br. 4
10² x 12²

BOOK

9' - 0" CLG.
DN

LINEN

Mbr.
13⁰ x 15⁰

10' - 0" CEILING

BOOK

Br. 3
10² x 12⁰

WHIRLPOOL

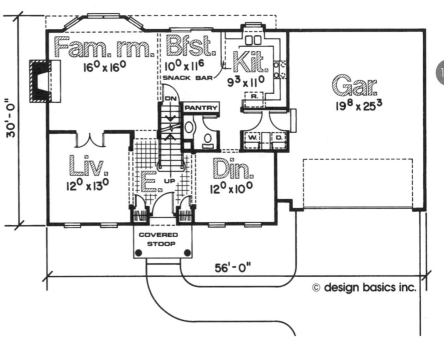

Fam. rm.
16⁰ x 16⁰

Bfst.
10⁰ x 11⁶

SNACK BAR

Kit.
9³ x 11⁰

R.

Gar.
19⁸ x 25³

DN

PANTRY

W. D.

Liv.
12⁰ x 13⁰

UP

Din.
12⁰ x 10⁰

30' - 0"

COVERED
STOOP

56' - 0"

© design basics inc.

199

Features

- Stately front elevation gives dynamic impact.
- Dramatic French doors connect formal living room and family room.
- Family room enhanced by raised hearth fireplace and bayed conversation area.
- Gourmet kitchen/breakfast area profits from extra-large pantry, two lazy Susans and patio door to the rear yard.

- Attractive stairway leads to second floor corridor with bookcase and large linen closet.
- Arrangement of secondary bedrooms gives privacy but remain within easy access to a roomy bath.
- Master suite enjoys volume ceiling, built-in bookcase and luxurious compartmented bath/dressing area.

First Floor	1,000 sq. ft.
Second Floor	993 sq. ft.
Total Living Area	1,993 sq. ft.

PRICE CODE: C

CUSTOMIZE IT!

ORDER TOLL FREE 1 ▪ 800 ▪ 533 ▪ 4350   24-HOUR FAX ORDERING 1 ▪ 800 ▪ 344 ▪ 4293

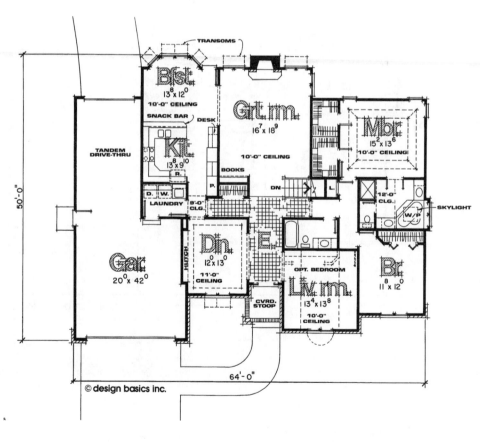

200

TRANSOMS

Bfst.
13⁸ x 12⁰
10'-0" CEILING

SNACK BAR

DESK

Grt.rm.
16⁷ x 18⁹

10'-0" CEILING

Mbr.
15² x 13⁶
10'-0" CEILING

BOOKS

Kit.
13⁰ x 9⁰

P.

DN

L.

12'-0"
CLG.

W/P

SKYLIGHT

D. W.

R.

LAUNDRY

9'-0"
CLG.

TANDEM
DRIVE-THRU

Dn.
12 x 13

E.

Gar.
20⁰ x 42⁰

11'-0"
CEILING

OPT. BEDROOM

Br.
11⁰ x 12

Liv. rm.
13⁴ x 13⁸

10'-0"
CEILING

CVRD.
STOOP

50'-0"

64'-0"

© design basics inc.

Features

- Hard surface trafficways.
- Formal dining room with hutch space and tiered ceiling up to 11-foot-high.
- Combination mud/laundry room for easy access from garage.
- Tandem 3-car drive-through garage.
- Efficient kitchen with snack bar and planning desk.
- Gorgeous fireplace surrounded by windows in great room with built-in bookcase and 10-foot ceiling.
- Skylit master bath with whirlpool, his and her vanities and plant ledge.
- His and her walk-in closets.
- Living room with volume ceiling can become third bedroom.

Total Living Area   **1,996 sq. ft.**

PRICE CODE: C

201

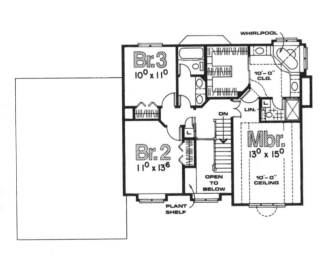

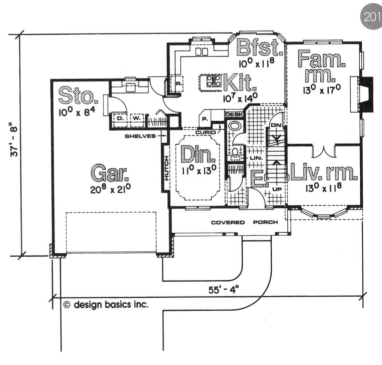

© design basics inc.

37' - 8"

55' - 4"

Features

- Distinctive design personality is complemented by large covered porch with wood railing.
- Living room is distinguished by warmth of bayed window and French doors leading to family room.
- Built-in curio cabinet adds interest to formal dining room.

- Large laundry room provides practical and desirable access from garage, outdoors and kitchen.
- Well-appointed kitchen with island cook top is planned to save you steps.
- Secondary bedrooms share comparmented hall bath.

First Floor	1,093 sq. ft.
Second Floor	905 sq. ft.
Total Living Area	1,998 sq. ft.

PRICE CODE: C

PLAN DB1380

202

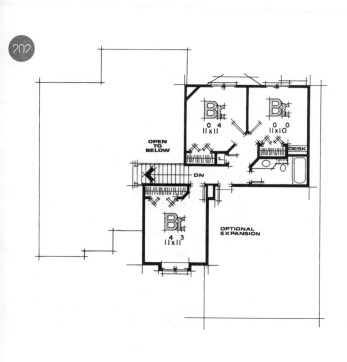

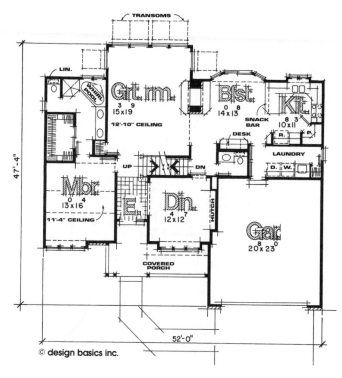

© design basics inc.

Features

- Inviting front porch welcomes guests.
- Hard-surfaced entryway is open to formal dining room with hutch space.
- Volume great room with generous windows and cozy, see-thru fireplace is open to entry.
- Main floor laundry area with coat closet and laundry sink doubles as mud entry from garage.

- Elegant sloped ceiling in master suite with pampering bath which includes double vanity, walk-in closet and window above the whirlpool tub.
- Future expansion possible over garage with access off hall.

First Floor	1,421 sq. ft.
Second Floor	578 sq. ft.
Total Living Area	1,999 sq. ft.

PRICE CODE: C

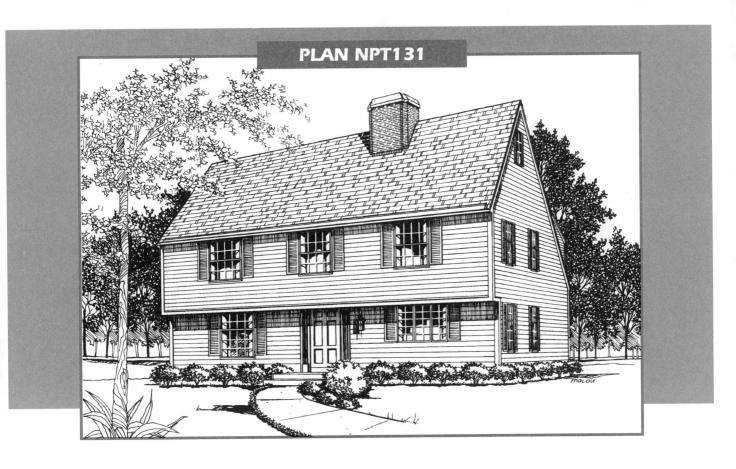

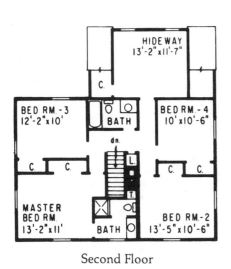

Second Floor

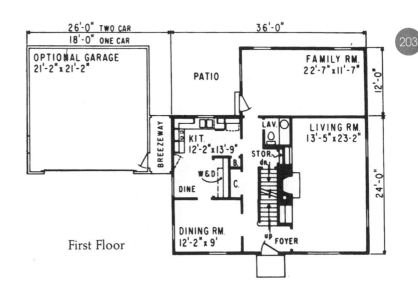

First Floor

Salt Box Settler

Features

- Traditional spirit of New England salt-box design is embodied in this home.
- Long living room with built-in shelves flanking the interior-wall fireplace occupies the right wing.
- Second-floor master bedroom includes master bath.
- Three additional bedrooms upstairs share a full bath.
- Hide-away room upstairs is perfect for quiet room or extra bedroom. Bonus room, 188 square feet.

First Floor	1,148 sq. ft.
Second Floor	864 sq. ft.
Bonus Room	188 sq. ft.
Total Living Area	2,200 sq. ft.

PRICE CODE: C

PLAN DB2361

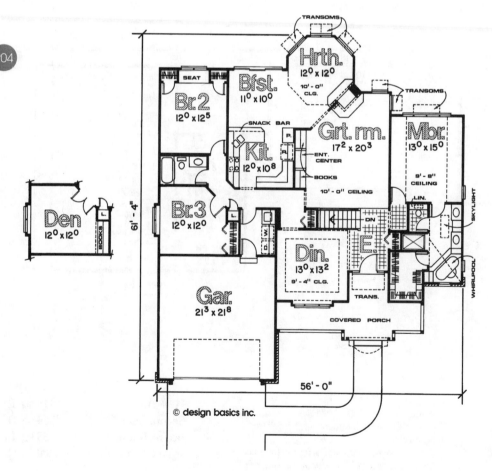

© design basics inc.

Features

- Elegant covered porch with arch above door adds romantic appeal to elevation.
- Formal dining room viewed from entry.
- Assets in ideal great room include 3-sided see-thru fireplace, entertainment center and bookcases.
- Bay windowed hearth room with 10-foot ceiling and see-thru fireplace offers a cozy retreat.
- Kitchen and dinette designed for livability with snack bar, pantry and ample counter space.
- Window seat framed by closets enhances bedroom #2; bedroom #3 can be converted to an optional den.
- Private master suite enjoys boxed ceiling, skylit dressing area with his and her lavs, corner whirlpool and large walk-in closet.

Total Living Area   2,015 sq. ft.

PRICE CODE: C

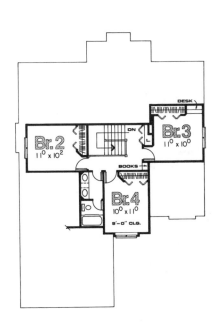

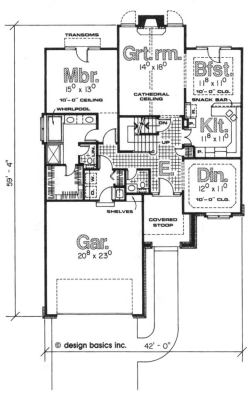

Features

- Gabled roof and limited brick use add affordability to this great elevation.
- Elegant U-stairs, French doors to kitchen and views to formal dining and great rooms create wonderful entry.
- Great room has cathedral ceiling, brick fireplace between large windows and direct access to breakfast area.
- Efficient kitchen offers corner sink, 2 pantries,

lazy Susan and snack bar.
- Large laundry with sink and closet.
- Master suite has atrium door to rear yard, great whirlpool bath with open shower and generous walk-in closet.
- Upstairs, 3 secondary bedrooms share compartmented bath.

First Floor	1,402 sq. ft.
Second Floor	617 sq. ft.
Total Living Area	2,019 sq. ft.

PRICE CODE: C

206

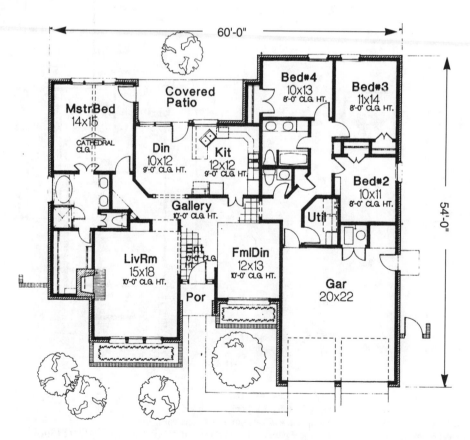

60'-0"

54'-0"

MstrBed
14x15
CATHEDRAL
CLG.

Covered
Patio

Bed#4
10x13
8'-0" CLG. HT.

Bed#3
11x14
8'-0" CLG. HT.

Din
10x12
9'-0" CLG. HT.

Kit
12x12
9'-0" CLG. HT.

Bed#2
10x11
8'-0" CLG. HT.

Gallery
10'-0" CLG. HT.

Util

LivRm
15x18
10'-0" CLG. HT.

Ent
10'-0" CLG. HT.

FmlDin
12x13
10'-0" CLG. HT.

Por

Gar
20x22

Total Living Area   2,030 sq. ft.

PRICE CODE: B

PLAN DB1769

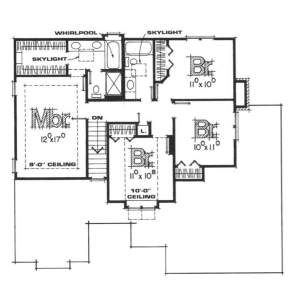

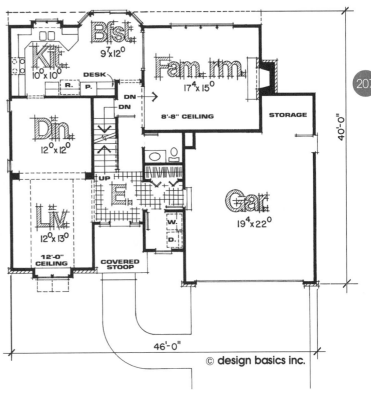

© design basics inc.

207

Features

- Large hall coat closet and nearby laundry room convenient to garage entrance into home.
- Volume living room opens to large dining room for entertaining.
- Efficient kitchen with pantry and planning desk open to bayed dinette.
- Sunken family room, private from entry, has fireplace and many windows.
- Extra storage space in garage.
- Secondary bedrooms segregated for privacy share skylit hall bath.
- Large master bedroom with elaborate skylit master bath includes walk-in closet, double vanity and compartmented stool and shower.

First Floor	1,081 sq. ft.
Second Floor	950 sq. ft.
Total Living Area	2,031 sq. ft.

PRICE CODE: C

PLAN FD8047-L

208

55'-0"

59'-10"

Bed#4
10x11

Din
12x9
9'-0" CLG. HT.

Patio

Bed#3
10x13

Kit
11x11
9'-0" CLG. HT.

10'-0" CLG. HT.

MstrBed
13x17
10'-0" CLG. HT.

Bed#2
11x12

FmlDin
10x12
10'-0" CLG. HT.

Gallery
TILE

Ent
TILE

Gar
29x21

Por

GreatRm
20x17
10'-0" CLG. HT.

Total Living Area   2,038 sq. ft.

PRICE CODE: B

C U S T O M I Z E   I T !

ORDER TOLL FREE   1 ▪ 800 ▪ 533 ▪ 4350   24-HOUR FAX ORDERING   1 ▪ 800 ▪ 344 ▪ 4293

PLAN JA5269

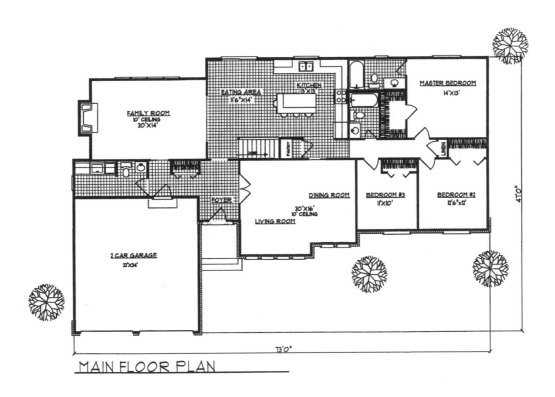

MAIN FLOOR PLAN

Total Living Area   2,042 sq. ft.

PRICE CODE: B

CUSTOMIZE IT!

ORDER TOLL FREE   1■800■533■4350   24-HOUR FAX ORDERING   1■800■344■4293

210

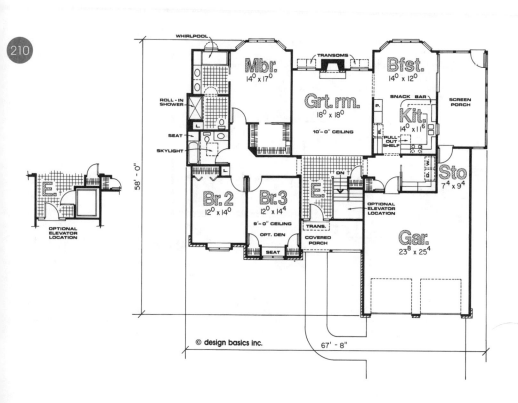

WHIRLPOOL

Mbr.
14⁰ x 17⁰

TRANSOMS

Bfst.
14⁰ x 12⁰

ROLL-IN
SHOWER

Grt. rm.
18⁰ x 18⁰

10'-0" CEILING

SNACK BAR

P.

SCREEN
PORCH

Kit.
14⁰ x 11⁶

SEAT

PULL-
OUT
SHELF

SKYLIGHT

Sto
7⁴ x 9⁴

Br. 2
12⁰ x 14⁰

Br. 3
12⁰ x 14⁴

E.

ON

OPTIONAL
ELEVATOR
LOCATION

9'-0" CEILING

OPT. DEN

TRANS.

COVERED
PORCH

Gar.
23⁸ x 25⁴

SEAT

© design basics inc.

58' - 0"

67' - 8"

E

OPTIONAL
ELEVATOR
LOCATION

Features

- Universally designed home.
- Arched details decorate this quaint ranch style home.
- Formal entry presents great room with brick fireplace, transoms and 10-foot-high ceiling.
- Spacious peninsula kitchen contains snack bar, pantry and pull-out shelf for extra counter space.
- Master suite features bayed window, roomy closet, dressing area, dual lavs, whirlpool bath and oversized shower.
- Bedroom #3 has window seat, 9-foot-high ceiling and can be an optional den.
- Stairs to basement have elevator option.

Total Living Area   2,053 sq. ft.

PRICE CODE: C

PLAN AM2212

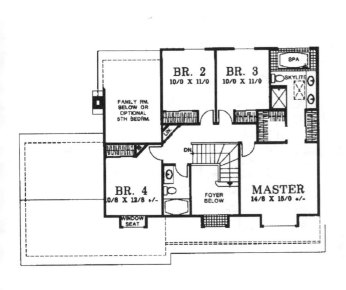

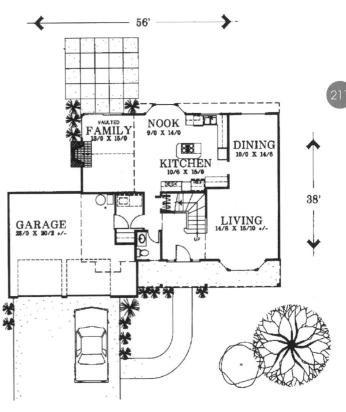

First Floor	1,105 sq. ft.
Second Floor	950 sq. ft.
Total Living Area	2,055 sq. ft.

PRICE CODE: B

Total Living Area   2,063 sq. ft.

PRICE CODE: B

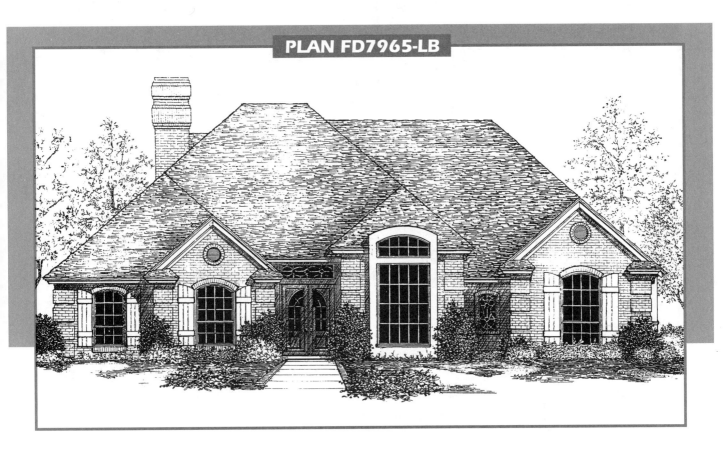

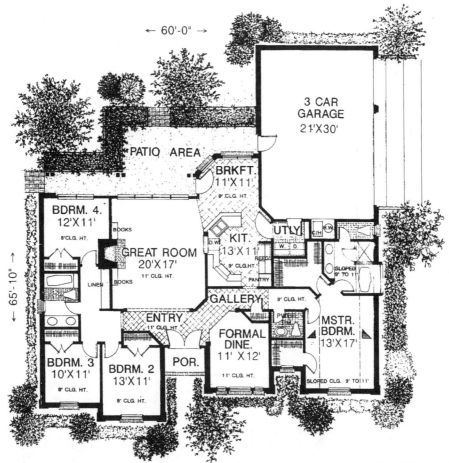

← 60'-0" →

65'-10"

3 CAR GARAGE
21'X30'

PATIO AREA

BRKFT.
11'X11'
8' CLG. HT.

BDRM. 4.
12'X11'
8'CLG. HT.

BOOKS

GREAT ROOM
20'X17'
11' CLG. HT.

BOOKS

LINEN

KIT.
13'X11'
9' CLG.HT.

UTLY

PANTRY

SLOPED
9' TO 1'

GALLERY

ENTRY
11' CLG. HT.

MSTR.
BDRM.
13'X17'

PWDR.

BDRM. 3
10'X11'
8' CLG. HT.

BDRM. 2
13'X11'
8' CLG. HT.

POR.

FORMAL
DINE.
11' X12'
11' CLG. HT.

SLOPED CLG. 9' TO 11'

Total Living Area   2,065 sq. ft.

PRICE CODE: B

CUSTOMIZE IT!

ORDER TOLL FREE   1■800■533■4350   24-HOUR FAX ORDERING   1■800■344■4293

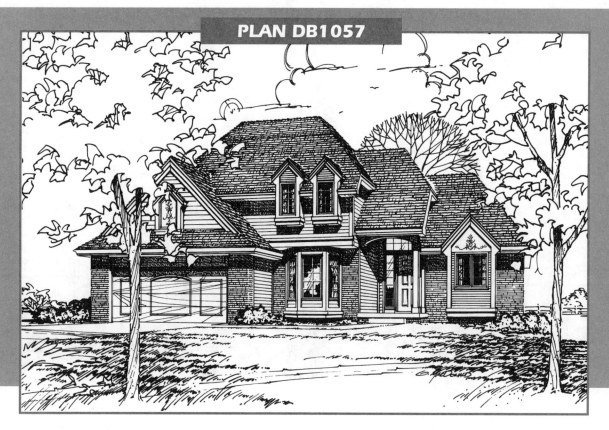

214

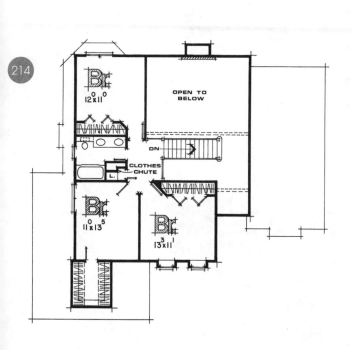

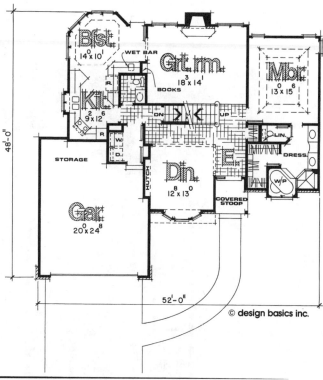

© design basics inc.

Features

- Formal dining room defined with columns open to entry.
- Dramatic open staircase.
- Efficient kitchen with pantry, corner range and wet bar/salad sink.
- Mud room/laundry at garage entry.
- Beautiful dinette with gazebo feeling.
- Volume ceiling in great room with fireplace framed

by windows.
- Master bedroom with deluxe bath area including double vanity, corner shower and whirlpool tub.
- Core hallway to secondary bedrooms.
- One secondary bedroom features walk-in closet.
- Centralized clothes chute and linen closet for upstairs bedrooms.

First Floor	1,348 sq. ft.
Second Floor	718 sq. ft.
Total Living Area	2,066 sq. ft.

PRICE CODE: C

PLAN DB1009

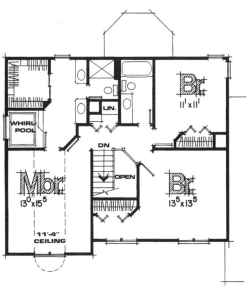

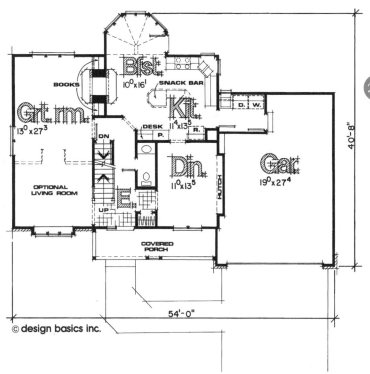

© design basics inc.

215

Features

- Hutch space in formal dining room off entry.
- Expansive great room with boxed window, see-thru fireplace and bookcases.
- Wall location provided for optional living room.
- Kitchen features island counter/snack bar, pantry, desk, fireplace and adjoining gazebo breakfast area.
- Garage with extra storage area accesses home

through laundry/mud room with utility sink.
- Master bedroom highlighted by volume ceiling and arched transom window.
- Master bath includes walk-in closet, his and her vanities and whirlpool tub.
- Secondary bedrooms share convenient hall bath.

First Floor	**1,096 sq. ft.**
Second Floor	**975 sq. ft.**
Total Living Area	**2,071 sq. ft.**

PRICE CODE: C

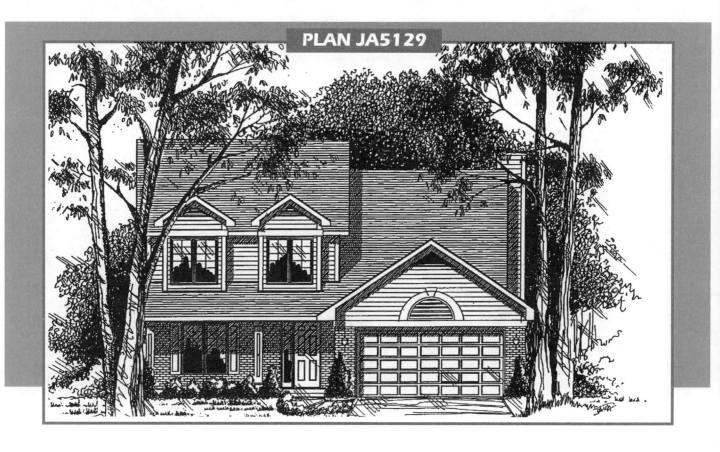

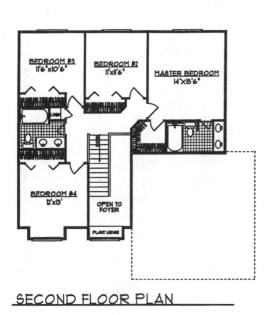

SECOND FLOOR PLAN

BEDROOM #3
11'6"x10'6"

BEDROOM #2
11'x11'6"

MASTER BEDROOM
14'x15'6"

BEDROOM #4
12'x13'

OPEN TO FOYER

PLANT LEDGE

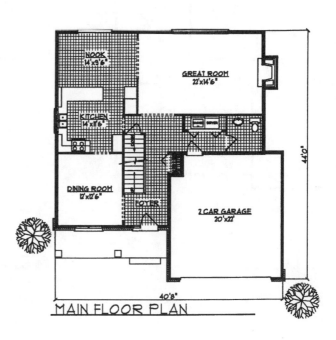

MAIN FLOOR PLAN

NOOK
14'x9'6"

GREAT ROOM
22'x14'6"

KITCHEN
14'x11'6"

DINING ROOM
12'x12'6"

FOYER

2 CAR GARAGE
20'x22'

44'0"

40'8"

First Floor	1,102 sq. ft.
Second Floor	971 sq. ft.
Total Living Area	2,073 sq. ft.

PRICE CODE: B

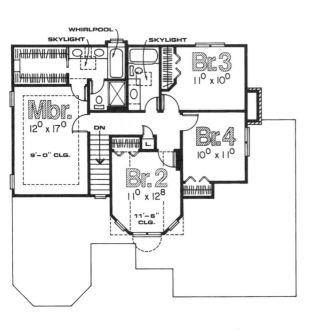

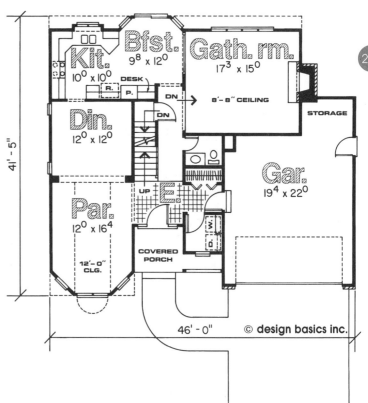

217

© design basics inc.

46' - 0"

Features

- Charming porch and arched windows of elevation allude to elegance within.
- Parlor with large bayed window and sloped ceiling harks back to simpler life.
- Formal dining area open to parlor invites entertaining with ease from kitchen.
- Bright kitchen and bayed breakfast area features

wrapping counters, pantry and desk.
- Step down into expansive gathering room with fireplace and abundant windows.
- Indulging master bedroom with skylit dressing area, dual lavs, whirlpool tub and large walk-in closet.

First Floor	1,113 sq. ft.
Second Floor	965 sq. ft.
Total Living Area	2,078 sq. ft.

PRICE CODE: C

CUSTOMIZE IT!

ORDER TOLL FREE 1▪800▪533▪4350   24-HOUR FAX ORDERING 1▪800▪344▪4293

PLAN AM2258B

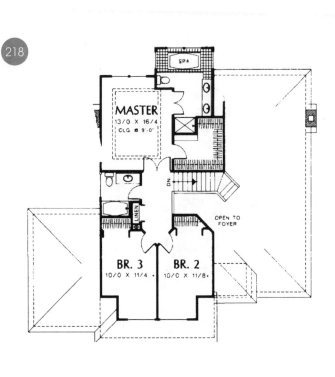

MASTER
13/0 X 16/4
(CLG. @ 9'-0")

BR. 3
10/0 X 11/4

BR. 2
10/0 X 11/8

SPA

LINEN

DN.

OPEN TO FOYER

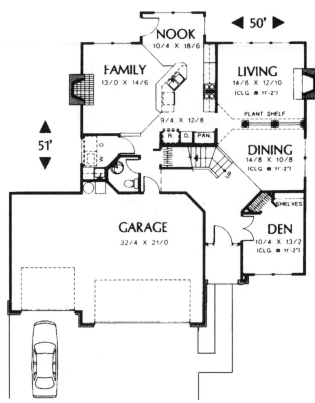

◀ 50' ▶

NOOK
10/4 X 18/6

FAMILY
13/0 X 14/6

LIVING
14/8 X 12/10
(CLG. @ 11'-2")

9/4 X 12/8

PLANT SHELF

51'

R. O. PAN.

DINING
14/8 X 10/8
(CLG. @ 11'-2")

W D

UP

SHELVES

GARAGE
32/4 X 21/0

DEN
10/4 X 13/2
(CLG. @ 11'-2")

First Floor	1,186 sq. ft.
Second Floor	895 sq. ft.
Total Living Area	2,081 sq. ft.

PRICE CODE: B

CUSTOMIZE IT!

ORDER TOLL FREE 1■800■533■4350   24-HOUR FAX ORDERING 1■800■344■4293

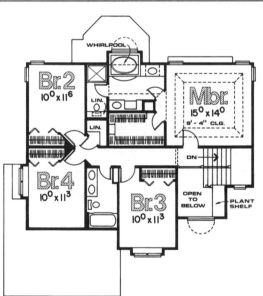

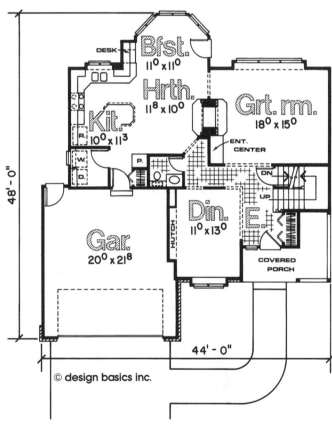

© design basics inc.

48' - 0"

44' - 0"

Br. 2 — 10⁰ x 11⁶
Br. 4 — 10⁰ x 11³
Br. 3 — 10⁰ x 11³
Mbr. — 15⁰ x 14⁰ — 9' - 4" CLG.
WHIRLPOOL
LIN.
DN
OPEN TO BELOW
PLANT SHELF

DESK
Bfst. — 11⁰ x 11⁰
Hrth. — 11⁸ x 10⁰
Kit. — 10⁰ x 11³
Grt. rm. — 18⁰ x 15⁰
ENT. CENTER
Gar. — 20⁰ x 21⁸
Din. — 11⁰ x 13⁰
HUTCH
COVERED PORCH
DN
UP
E.
P.

Features

- 2-story entry open to interesting staircase and formal dining room with boxed window and hutch space.
- Great room with large windows, entertainment center and see-thru fireplace.
- Hearth room takes advantage of see-thru fireplace.
- Island counter, desk and pantry in kitchen open to bayed dinette.
- Vaulted ceiling and unique angle into walk-in closet and dressing area make this a special master suite.
- Irresistible oval whirlpool under arched window and his and her vanities in master bath/dressing area.

First Floor	1,062 sq. ft.
Second Floor	1,023 sq. ft.
Total Living Area	2,085 sq. ft.

PRICE CODE: C

CUSTOMIZE IT!

ORDER TOLL FREE 1 ▪ 800 ▪ 533 ▪ 4350   24-HOUR FAX ORDERING 1 ▪ 800 ▪ 344 ▪ 4293

PLAN FD8162-L

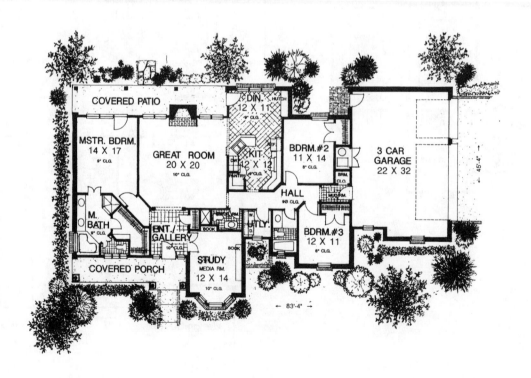

Total Living Area   2,086 sq. ft.

PRICE CODE: B

221

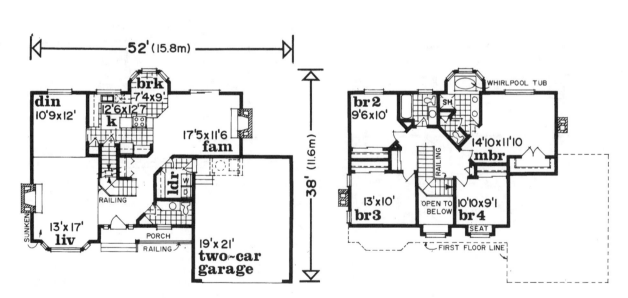

First Level 1062 square feet   Second Level 1026 square feet

Features

- Dormer window brightens foyer and open staircase.
- Sunken living room boasts bay window and masonry fireplace.
- Kitchen, with centre cooking island, is open to breakfast bay and family room.

- Family room has masonry fireplace and sliding glass walk-through to patio.
- Master bedroom features walk-in closet and lavish ensuite.
- Ensuite features spa, tucked in windowed-bay, twin vanity and shower.

Total Living Area   2,088 sq. ft.

PRICE CODE: B

CUSTOMIZE IT!

ORDER TOLL FREE   1 ▪ 800 ▪ 533 ▪ 4350   24-HOUR FAX ORDERING   1 ▪ 800 ▪ 344 ▪ 4293

222

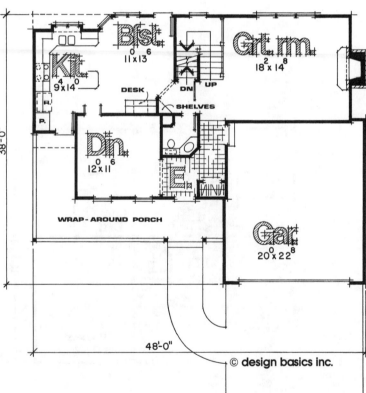

© design basics inc.

Features

- Main level footage optimized and second level footage maximized.
- Private door onto spacious wrap-around porch from kitchen.
- Large kitchen includes pantry, island counter, roll-top desk and lazy Susan.
- Convenient main floor powder bath.
- Great room opens to staircase at the rear brightened with window on landing.

- Double doors to large master bedroom.
- Deluxe master bath area with whirlpool, transom windows and sloped ceiling.
- Laundry room with soaking sink on same level as bedrooms.
- 3 linen closets on second level.
- Secondary bedrooms share centrally located bath with double vanity.

First Floor	927 sq. ft.
Second Floor	1,163 sq. ft.
Total Living Area	2,090 sq. ft.

PRICE CODE: C

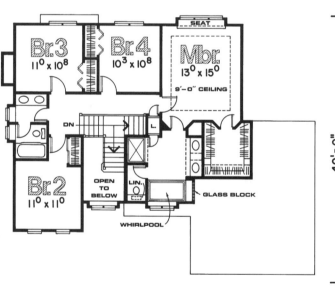

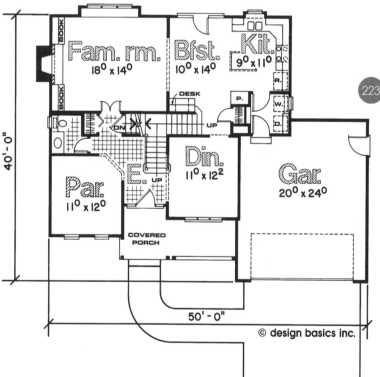

223

© design basics inc.

Features

- Covered porch invites you into this country style home.
- Handsome bookcases frame fireplace in spacious family room.
- Double doors off entry provide family room added privacy.
- Kitchen features island, lazy Susan and easy access

to walk-in laundry.
- Master bedroom features boxed ceiling and separate entries into walk-in closet and master bath.
- Upstairs, hall bath is compartmentalized, allowing maximum usage for today's busy families.

First Floor	1,082 sq. ft.
Second Floor	1,021 sq. ft.
Total Living Area	2,103 sq. ft.

PRICE CODE: C

CUSTOMIZE IT!

ORDER TOLL FREE 1▪800▪533▪4350   24-HOUR FAX ORDERING 1▪800▪344▪4293

224

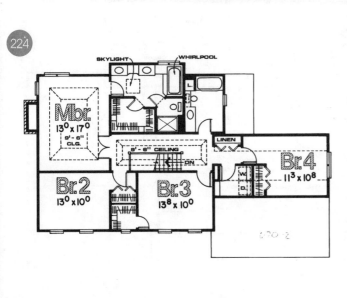

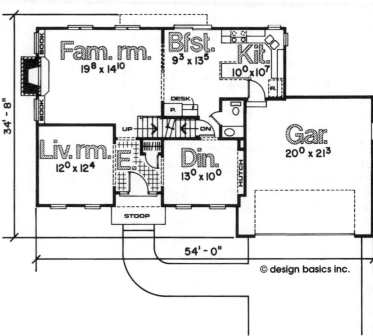

© design basics inc.

Features

- Bright entry open to living room and formal dining room with hutch space.
- Large family room boasts stunning fireplace framed by built-in bookcases and awning windows above.
- Direct access from garage into kitchen including corner sink with windows above, island and pantry.
- Sunny breakfast area includes planning desk.
- Master bedroom with vaulted ceiling.
- Master bath features skylit dressing area, whirlpool, double lavs and walk-in closet.
- Convenient second floor laundry.

First Floor	998 sq. ft.
Second Floor	1,206 sq. ft.
Total Living Area	2,204 sq. ft.

PRICE CODE: D